GW01395947

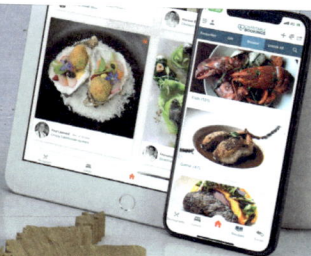

For the full collection visit
charitablebookings.com/recipe-books

CHARITABLE **BOOKINGS**

SIGNATURE♥DISH

USA

To:

From:

Message:

3 STEPS TO UNLOCK YOUR 250 U.S. RECIPES

1 Download the free **CHARITABLE BOOKINGS** lifestyle app.

2 Go to 📖 *Recipes*, tap on **501-750**, then tap on **Unlock.**

3 Enter the **unique code** to unlock these 250 **CHARITABLE BOOKINGS** Signature Dish USA main course recipes and, in addition, a donation will be made by **CHARITABLE BOOKINGS** to a charity of your choice at absolutely no cost to you.

SCRATCH OFF TO REVEAL

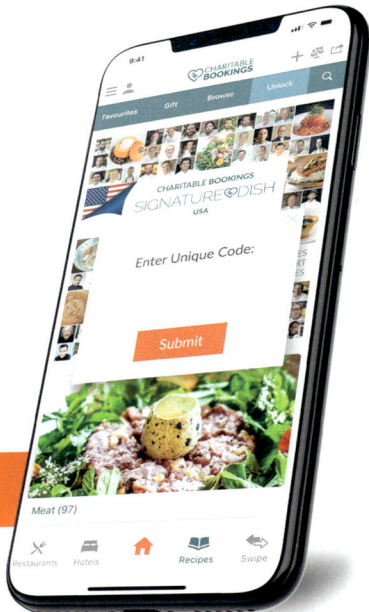

Download on the **App Store**

GET IT ON **Google Play**

CHARITABLE BOOKINGS

Foreword

It is my pleasure to write the foreword to this wonderful recipe book collection that showcases 1,500 of the best loved chefs working at the finest restaurants, private members clubs and 5* hotels throughout the U.K. and America, while knowing that together we are all helping to support countless deserving causes.

In an increasingly cashless society we set up the lifestyle restaurant and hotel reservations platform, CHARITABLE **BOOKINGS**, as a simple way to help charities generate additional unrestricted funds and awareness at no cost to themselves, while continuing our ethos of encouraging individuals and organisations to support good causes as part of their daily life.

Individuals can choose from thousands of U.K. and U.S. registered charities who are supported by CHARITABLE **BOOKINGS** every time they eat out or book a hotel. This costs the individual and the charity nothing and we hope that this will become an essential free tool to help charities boost their bottom line and to enable corporate organisations to increase the funds they generate for good causes. Of course, we are indebted to the support from our many thousands of restaurant and hotel partners who will help make a real difference to the lives of those in need both now and in the future.

With so many excellent restaurants and hotels on board we decided to showcase some of the chefs in what was planned as a small section on our app and website. The response from chefs and restaurants was so overwhelming that we made the decision to publish our first CHARITABLE **BOOKINGS** recipe book. We have now gone on to create a collection of books, each unlocking 250 recipes on the lifestyle app.

We hope you will enjoy these delightful books in the knowledge that every copy has generated funds for good causes.

Having encouraged you to cook at home with these books and via the app, we would now like to encourage you to go out and eat. Use CHARITABLE **BOOKINGS** for your personal and business restaurant bookings and help us support the restaurant industry and the causes dear to your heart, making a positive difference to those less fortunate.

It's very easy to use and you can select a different charity to benefit every time you go out – with it costing you absolutely nothing to do so!

I hope you enjoy the book collection and download all the recipes. Thank you again for supporting those wonderful organisations that do so much good for so many.

Lord Fink

Editor's welcome

Welcome to the CHARITABLE **BOOKINGS** Signature Dish recipe book collection, an initiative of CHARITABLE **BOOKINGS** that aims to support up to 500,000 U.K. & U.S. registered causes.

Firstly, I would like to take this opportunity to dedicate these books to my late father, Michael, who continues to inspire and motivate me and taught me to appreciate great ingredients, the importance of tunnel vision and to always try to do good by others.

With this in mind I decided I wanted to do something different, something big, that hadn't been attempted before. I wanted to bring together a wide variety of the best loved chefs from the world's leading restaurants, private members clubs and 5* hotels, in support of thousands of charities, while creating the perfect gift for all foodies. The huge number of recipes available within this collection shows you really can't judge a book by its cover!

Compiling this collection to date has been a massive undertaking, but it has been an enjoyable journey, allowing me to bring together a selection of 1,500 mouth-watering main course signature dish recipes through the collection for you to enjoy at home. From simple hearty meals and exotic spicy creations, to Michelin star wonders and dinner party crowd pleasers, we have assembled a fantastic array of delicious restaurant quality recipes to give everyone the opportunity to cook like a professional chef.

What makes these cook books different is that not only can you be inspired by the wonderful array of recipes, but by simply downloading the free CHARITABLE **BOOKINGS** lifestyle app and entering the unique code found at the front of each book, you will unlock 250 recipes for you to access from your iOS, Android smart phones or tablet.

This ever growing book collection is a perfect complement to the CHARITABLE **BOOKINGS** lifestyle, restaurant and hotel booking platform. Allowing you to not only enjoy fantastic benefits, but to also raise unrestricted funds for a charity of your choice every time you make either a hotel booking or restaurant reservation via the app or charitable**bookings**.com, at absolutely no cost to you.

Each chef's dish will not only brighten up your table, but will help brighten up the lives of people who need help and support. By entering the unique code found at front of this book, a donation will be made by CHARITABLE **BOOKINGS** to a charity of your choice at absolutely no cost to you. A delicious way to support good causes.

We hope you'll find some exciting recipes here to try and with any luck you will buy these books as a gift for your family members, friends and colleagues, so all the foodies you know can enjoy these delicious inspiring recipes and this ever growing worldwide philanthropic collaboration.

David Johnstone
Editor-In-Chief

500 LEADING CHEFS' SIGNATURE DISH RECIPES FROM THE FOUR CORNERS OF THE UNITED KINGDOM...

Each of the two U.K. volumes of the CHARITABLE BOOKINGS Signature Dish recipe book collection unlocks **250** mouth-watering dishes from **250** of the leading chefs from the finest restaurants, private members' clubs and 5* hotels throughout the four corners of the United Kingdom.

Each book contains 50 recipes and a **unique code** that unlocks all **250** on the free CHARITABLE BOOKINGS lifestyle app. On entering the **unique code** you will also have the opportunity to select a cause close to your heart, from a growing list of over 500,000 U.K. & U.S. registered charities, CHARITABLE BOOKINGS will make a donation to that cause at absolutely no cost to you.

charitable**bookings**.com/**recipe-books**

CHARITABLE **BOOKINGS**

SIGNATURE♡DISH

UK

1,000 LEADING CHEFS' SIGNATURE DISH RECIPES FROM ACROSS ALL 50 STATES OF AMERICA...

Each of the four U.S. volumes of the CHARITABLE BOOKINGS Signature Dish recipe book collection unlocks **250** mouth-watering dishes from **250** of the leading chefs from the finest restaurants and 5* hotels from across all 50 states of America.

Each book contains 50 recipes and a **unique code** that unlocks all **250** on the free CHARITABLE BOOKINGS lifestyle app. On entering the **unique code** you will also have the opportunity to select a cause close to your heart, from a growing list of over 500,000 U.K. & U.S. registered charities, CHARITABLE BOOKINGS will make a donation to that cause at absolutely no cost to you.

charitablebookings.com/**recipe-books**

CHARITABLE **BOOKINGS**

SIGNATURE DISH

USA

10 | charitablebookings.com

L♥VE...

CHARITABLE BOOKINGS is the FREE lifestyle app that has fantastic benefits and also gives back to your favourite charity at absolutely no cost to you.

CHARITABLE BOOKINGS

charitablebookings.com

Download on the App Store

GET IT ON Google Play

Book at over 8,500 restaurants across the U.K. and £1/$1 will be donated for EVERY diner, by CHARITABLE BOOKINGS, to a charity of your choice at absolutely no cost to you.

"ingenious"
Sunday Times Magazine

"ethical eating"
Daily Mail

L♥VE...

Book at over 250,000 hotels across the world and CHARITABLE BOOKINGS will donate £1/$1 per guest for EVERY night's stay to a charity of your choice at absolutely no cost to you.

"Unlike any other online UK booking platform"

Institute of Fundraising

Enjoy access to 1,000s of Secret Tips including the best restaurant table numbers to ask for when making a booking.

"Everyone is able to support charitable fundraising while dining out at absolutely no cost to themselves. Charity just got so much easier"

Style

L♥VE...

Enjoy Deals at selected restaurants including a complimentary round of drinks for you and all your friends.

"This could be the most enjoyable and easiest way to do good"
ELLE Decoration

Enjoy collecting Loyalty Points on selected restaurant and hotel bookings and redeeming them for gifts and rewards or donate them to a charity of your choice.

"Good deeds you can do.. No 1"
Evening Standard

L♥VE...

Enjoy reading free articles on the go from the worlds of luxury and philanthropy.

"Pick of the best"

Exclusively British

Enjoy free recipes EVERY week from the CHARITABLE BOOKINGS Signature Dish cookbook collection, created by 1,500 of the best loved chefs from the U.K.'s & U.S.'s leading restaurants, private members clubs and 5* hotels.

"Very, very special"
COUNTRY LIFE

L♥VE...

"Website of the week"
The SUN

Enjoy playing Swipe daily for free for the chance to WIN money for your favourite charity and individual prizes worth up to £7,500/$10,000 at the world's most luxurious brands including: Harrods, Agent Provocateur, Louboutin, Gucci, Dunhill, Prada, Cartier and many more.

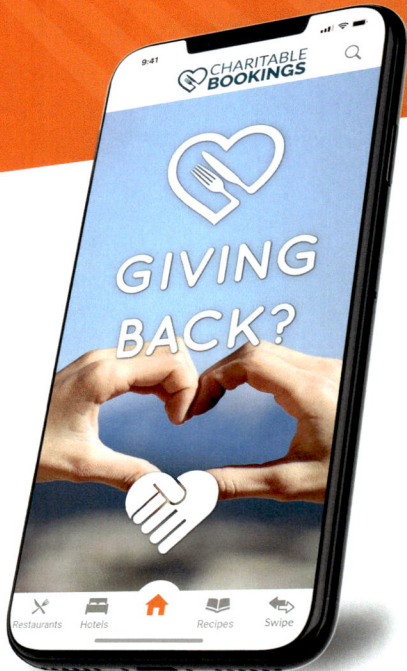

Enjoy Giving Back for FREE to a cause close to your heart from a growing list of over 500,000 U.K. and U.S. registered charities by using the CHARITABLE BOOKINGS lifestyle app today.

"A way in which to help thousands of people less fortunate, through a simple everyday thing"

Made in Shoreditch

250 CHEFS

and a selection of

50 RECIPES

Browse the following pages to preview a selection of 50 Signature Dish recipes ready for you to try.

Use the **unique code** at the beginning of this book to unlock the **250** Signature Dish main course recipes on the free CHARITABLE **BOOKINGS** lifestyle app.

CHARITABLE BOOKINGS

Download on the App Store

GET IT ON Google Play

	Nicolas Abello	*L'Appart*	Black sea bass with cobalt and dragon carrots, and grapefruit
	Vartan Abgaryan	*71 Above*	Summer squash poblano with cilantro, peanut, white soy, scallion, risotto stuffed blossom
	Kaleo Adams	*Polo Lounge at The Beverly Hills Hotel*	16oz Bone in NY strip with carrot-citrus puree, romanesco, spring onion and beef jus
	Fabrizio Aielli	*Sea Salt*	Lobster risotto
	Robert Aikens	*Espita Mezcaleria*	Lamb neck and ribs enfrijoladas, with house made lamb chorizo and cumin yoghurt tetela
	Karen Akunowicz	*Myers + Chang*	Pan-roasted soy-glazed salmon with Cool Cucumber Salad
	Stephanie Alderete	*Nikolai's Roof*	Magret duck breast with toasted coconut farro and blueberry nuoc cham
	Kim Alter	*Nightbird*	Quail egg with brown butter hollandaise and fried leek
	Paul Anders	*Sweet Basil*	Grilled wagyu ribeye filet with charred broccolini, salt roasted potato, Umbrian olive oil and salsa verde
	Michael Annandono	*Michaelangelo's*	Tortellini di vitello con prosciutto e piselli

Foodie fact #1
Avocado has highest protein
content of all fruit.

Vartan Abgaryan - *71 Above*
Summer squash poblano with cilantro, peanut, white soy, scallion, risotto stuffed blossom
Unlock these 250 recipes on the free CHARITABLE BOOKINGS lifestyle app.

NICOLAS ABELLO
L'Appart

BLACK SEA BASS with cobalt and dragon carrots, and grapefruit
SERVES 4 | PREPARATION TIME 1 HOUR 30 MINUTES | COOKING TIME 50 MINUTES

Equipment
juicer
vitamix
For the Dish
400g (*14 oz*) black sea bass
olive oil, to fry
salt and timut pepper
micro parsley

For the Mousseline
2.7kg (*6 lbs*) carrots loose,
reserve some uncooked for
vinaigrette
½ sweet onion
200g (*7 oz*) crystallized ginger
480g (*17 oz*) heavy cream
480g (*17 oz*) whole milk
fleur de sel and timut pepper
170g (*6 oz*) salted butter

For the Vinaigrette
212g (*7.5 oz*) mascarpone
13g (*0.45 oz*) olive oil
10g (*0.35 oz*) Dijon mustard
2 limes, juiced
1 ruby red grapefruit
For the Carrots
226g (*½ lb*) cobalt and dragon
carrots or baby orange carrots,
mixed
olive oil, to roast
fleur de sel and timut pepper

To prepare the dish, start by cleaning the skin of the fish. Remove the scales and season with salt, pepper and olive oil. Leave in the fridge.

To make the carrot mousseline, wash and peel the loose carrots. Cut into pieces and also cut the sweet onion. Start to melt the salted butter in a pot then add the onion, carrot - reserve some for the vinaigrette - and the ginger. Season with salt, add your heavy cream and milk and simmer. Blend your cooked carrot, your mousseline needs to be fine. Rectify the seasoning.

To make the vinaigrette, place the rest of the carrot in the juicer, reduce the juice by half and add the mascarpone, olive oil, Dijon mustard and lime juice. Cut the grapefruit into segments.

Peel the roasting carrots and cook them in an oven at 150°C (*300°F*), with olive oil, salt and timut pepper until they are tender.

To finish and serve, cook your fish in a pan. Fry with the skin side facing the pan in olive oil. Finish with salted butter. Add the carrot mousseline on the plate, the vinaigrette and grapefruit, the cooked fish, baby carrots and micro parsley then finish with some timut pepper.

KALEO ADAMS
Polo Lounge at The Beverly Hills Hotel

16oz BONE IN NY STRIP with carrot-citrus purée, romanesco, spring onion and beef jus
SERVES 4 | PREPARATION TIME 1 HOUR 30 MINUTES | COOKING TIME 5 HOURS

Equipment
Thermomix

For the Carrot Citrus Purée
2kg (*70 oz*) red carrots
100g (*3.5 oz*) butter
100g (*3.5 oz*) Minneola
tangerine juice
7 lbs butter, melted

For the Beef Jus
2.2kg (*5 lbs*) beef scrap, cubed
3 tbsp olive oil
½ cup onion
½ cup celery
½ cup carrots
1 bunch of thyme
12 black peppercorn

6 bottles red burgundy wine
4.5l (*1 gallon*) rich chicken stock
¼ cup red wine vinegar
¼ cup honey
For the Garnish
5 grilled spring onions
7 small pieces of romanesco
finishing salt

To make the carrot-citrus puree, heat the oven to 150°C (*300°F*). Melt the butter in a pot large enough to hold the carrots. It should melt but not foam. Peel the carrots and submerge into the melted butter. Place rondeau in oven and cook for 2 hours. Take the carrots out of the butter and purée in a Thermomix for 30 minutes with the tangerine juice and cold butter.

To prepare the dish, first preheat the oven to 190°C (*375°F*). Reduce the wine by approximately 40%. In a separate pot, reduce the chicken stock by approximately 40%. Heat a large rondeau. Add oil and allow to get smoking hot. Add the beef scraps so there is an even, single layer and brown on all sides. Do in batches, if necessary, without burning the bottom of the pan. Remove all beef from the pan and drain. Add the mirepoix to the pan and roast. Add honey and cook. Deglaze with red wine vinegar. Add reduced red wine and reduced chicken stock. Place entire rondeau in oven for 3 hours, stirring occasionally. Strain through a fine mesh strainer. Reduce until desired consistency and flavor is obtained.

To finish and plate, cook the NY steak over charcoal to the desired temperature. Allow to rest 2 minutes. Using a small offset spatula, spread the purée on the left side of the plate. Place the spring onion and Romanesco on the purée. Place the beef on the right side of the plate. Preferably pour the sauce tableside. If not, sauce between the steak and the purée.

	Michael Anthony	*Gramercy Tavern*	Roasted delicata squash with chicories, hazelnuts and pears
	Diane Anthony	*Ten Degrees South*	Bobotie
	Julien Asseo	*Guy Savoy Caesar Palace*	Crispy line-caught sea bass with delicate spices
	Michele Baldacci	*Locanda Vini e Olii*	Peposo alla fornacina.
	Benjamin Balesteri	*Poggio Trattoria*	Grilled Mt Lassen trout with butter beans, asparagus, castelvetrano olives and preserved lemon
	Jeff Balfour	*Southerleigh Fine Food & Brewery*	Braised oxtail sopes
	Robert Barrera	*Cane & Canoe*	Seared ahi tuna and molokai sweet potato with ali'i mushrooms, snap peas and tomatoes
	Matthew Basford	*Canoe*	Slow roasted Carolina rabbit
	Lidia Bastianich	*Lidia's*	Roasted loin of pork stuffed with prunes
	Emma Bengtsson	*Aquavit*	Sirloin and cabbage

Foodie fact #2
The first ice cream cone was
created at the St Louis World's
Fair of 1904.

Robert Aikens - *Espita Mezcaleria*

Lamb neck and ribs enfrijoladas, with house made lamb chorizo and cumin yoghurt tetela

Unlock these 250 recipes on the free CHARITABLE BOOKINGS lifestyle app.

KIM ALTER
Nightbird

QUAIL EGG with brown butter hollandaise and fried leek
SERVES 10 | PREPARATION TIME 10 MINUTES | COOKING TIME 10 MINUTES

For the Dish
10 pack quail eggs
1 bag large leeks
120ml (*½ cup*) white wine
1 shallot, sliced
3 sprigs tarragon

1 tbsp black peppercorn
3 egg yolks
375g (*1½ cup*) brown butter
1 tsp salt
fleur de sel, to garnish
480g (*2 cups*) rice oil, to fry

To prepare the dish, preheat the oven to 120°C (*250°F*). Clean and chiffonade (*slice finely*) the large leeks, discarding the green and only using the tops (*white*). Boil 6 cups of water and then pour the hot water over the leeks and let sit for about 5 minutes. Drain and place on a half sheet tray with multifolds underneath. Place in an oven for approximately 5 minutes to dry out. In a medium pot, bring 10 cups of generously salted water to a boil. Make an ice bath to cool the eggs quickly after cooked. Place the quail eggs in the boiling water for 2 minutes and 15 seconds. Take out and put into the ice bath. Once cooled, peel. Reserve the eggs in a warm place. A great tip is to use the egg crate that the quail eggs came in and store them in that once peeled.

Now, in a small pot, add the shallot, tarragon, peppercorns and white wine. Bring to a boil and reduce the heat and continue reducing by 1/2. This will be your base for the hollandaise. To make the brown butter, place the butter in a pan. Once the butter starts to smell nutty and turn brown, strain. In a blender, add the egg yolks and run the blender for about 1 minute. Add the white wine reduction. Add salt. Slowly start to strain in the butter as the blender is still on until you have a thick emulsified sauce. Taste and season. To fry the leek, bring the oil up to 190°C (*375°F*) and put the leeks in a pot. Once the leeks start to look crisp and lightly turn brown take them out and place onto a pad to soak out the grease. Season with salt.

To finish and serve, take a small ramekin and make a bed for the quail egg in the fried leeks. Place the quail egg in the center and season with fleur de sel. Put a nice dollop of brown butter hollandaise in the center of the egg. All these items should be made day of for best results. All items should be warm.

MICHAEL ANNANDONO

Michaelangelo's

TORTELLINI DI VITELLO con prosciutto e piselli
SERVES 4 | PREPARATION TIME 5 MINUTES | COOKING TIME 20 MINUTES

For the Dish
2 tbsp butter
75g (½ cup) Prosciutto di Parma, sliced and cut into strips
60g (¼ cup) chicken stock
720g (3 cups) heavy whipping cream
80g (½ cup) green peas, frozen

60g (½ cup) Parmigiano Reggiano, grated
sea salt and black pepper, to taste
453g (1 lb) veal tortellini, cooked, or any other stuffed pasta
2 tbsp sea salt

To prepare the dish, take a medium stock pot and boil 3 quarts of water and add 2 tbsp of sea salt. Cook the tortellini or other pasta until al dente. In a medium sauce pan, melt the butter and render Prosciutto until slightly crisp. Add stock and deglaze. Pour in heavy cream, boil and reduce until thick. Add peas and grated Parmigiano Reggiano. Add sea salt and black pepper to taste. Mix with cooked pasta and serve.

Garnish with shaved Parmigiano Reggiano and fresh basil sprig.

	Jon Bennell	*Bonnell's*	White gazpacho with lump crab
Matthew Bernero	*Minetta Tavern*	Roasted Long Island duck breast
Fredrik Berselius	*Aska*	Small bird aged for two weeks and roasted in a juniper and foaming butter with preserved berries and fruit
Austin Blaize	*Forks & Corks*	Bronzed redfish with Louisiana crawfish tails in a sweet pepper and brown butter vinaigrette, with wild rice blend, haricot verts and toasted pecans
Richard Blondin	*The Refectory*	Baby rack of lamb
Aaron Bludorn	*Cafe Boulud*	Stripped bass "en paupiette"
Edward Bolus	*Mill's Tavern*	Kibbeh nayyeh
Daniel Boulud	*db Bistro*	Coq au vin
James Boyce	*Cotton Row*	Braised beef short rib in red wine and pomegranate
Jared Braithwaite	*Colonie*	Campanelle with peconic escargot with garlic, pecorino, orange and mint

Foodie fact #3
The first grocery product to use bar codes was Wrigleys chewing gum.

Karen Akunowicz - *Myers + Chang*
Pan-roasted soy-glazed salmon with cool cucumber salad
Unlock these 250 recipes on the free CHARITABLE BOOKINGS lifestyle app.

DANIEL BOULUD
db Bistro

COQ AU VIN
SERVES 8 | PREPARATION TIME 25 MINUTES + THE DAY BEFORE | COOKING TIME 2 HOURS

Equipment
butchers twine
cheesecloth

For the Dish
8 chicken legs
1 medium onions, sliced
1 carrot, sliced
2 celery stalks, sliced
2 heads garlic, sliced in half
1 sachet made of 8 sprigs of thyme, 1 fresh bay leaf, 2 tsp coriander seed, 1 tsp cracked white pepper tied up in cheesecloth with butchers twine
900g (*2 lbs*) small button mushrooms, cleaned and trimmed
450g (*1 lb*) pearl onions
450g (*1 lb*) slab bacon, sliced

1 bottle (*750ml*) dry red wine
½ bottle (*375 ml*) ruby port wine
4 tbsp olive oil
4 tbsp all-purpose flour
480g (*2 cups*) unsalted chicken stock or canned chicken broth
480g (*2 cups*) unsalted veal stock
salt and freshly ground pepper

Start preparing the dish a day before by separating the chicken legs and thighs. Place in a large container with the onion, carrot, celery, garlic and sachet. Cook the bacon in a large sauté pan over medium high heat until just crispy. Wrap the bacon, pearl onions, and mushrooms in separate cheesecloth bundles and tie with the butchers twine; add to the container with the chicken. Cover all ingredients with the red wine and port, marinate in the refrigerator overnight.

Now get ready to cook the dish by preheating the oven to 160°C (*325°F*). Drain all ingredients from the wine and reserve. Reduce the wine in a large pot by half. Meanwhile, pat the chicken dry, season well, and heat the olive oil over medium high heat in a large Dutch oven. Sear the chicken on all sides in one layer. Remove the chicken; add the sliced vegetables and cook, stirring occasionally, on medium heat until soft, about 6 minutes. Add the flour and cook, stirring, for another 4 minutes.

To cook and finish off, add the reduced wine, chicken, mushroom, pearl onion and bacon bundles to the Dutch oven with the veal and chicken stock. Bring to a simmer, cover with a round of parchment paper and transfer to the oven. Cook for 1 to 1 1/2 hours, or until the chicken is tender. Strain the chicken and vegetables from the sauce, discarding the sliced carrot, onion and celery. Remove the bacon, pearl onion and mushroom from their bundles. If the sauce seems too thin, return to the heat and reduce until desired consistency: it should coat the back of a spoon. Incorporate all ingredients back together and serve hot.

NELLY BULEJE
Metropolitan at The 9

BRANZINO DISH
SERVES 2 | PREPARATION TIME 45 MINUTES | COOKING TIME 20 MINUTES

For the Pomegranate Glaze
13g (*0.5 oz*) pomegranate paste
27g (*1 oz*) pomegranate juice

For the Dish
microgreens
½ lemon

For the Tomato Relish
12 havles of halved cherry
tomatoes 1 tbsp basil, fresh,
chiffonade
1 tbsp tarragon, fresh, chopped
½ tsp red wine vinegar
½ tsp extra virgin olive oil
½ tsp garlic, minced
½ tsp shallot, minced

For the Branzino
1 tsp Kosher salt
½ tsp ground black pepper
½ tsp garlic, minced
½ tsp shallots
½ fresh orange
3 star anise
1 tbsp olive oil

First make the pomegranate glaze by adding the ingredients to a bowl and whisking until fully combined.

Now make the tomato relish by adding the ingredients to a metal bowl and gently tossing with a spoon.

To cook the fish, season both sides and the inside with Kosher salt and fresh cracked black pepper. After seasoning, put the chopped garlic, shallots and squeezed orange juice inside the clean and scaled fish. Transfer to a lightly oiled roasting pan, and place 3 pieces of star anise over the top and drizzle 1 tbsp of olive oil before placing in the oven for 15 to 20 minutes. When ready the outer silver part of the fish will have become a light brown with a crisp feel to the touch and the inside meat will have transformed from clear to a rich, flaky opaque. Allow to rest for 3 minutes so that all the meat regains its moistness.

Transfer to the plate using a fish spatula. Squeeze half a lemon onto the fish, drizzle the pomegranate glaze over the top, evenly lay the tomato relish over fish and garnish with micro greens.

	Sean Brock	*Husk*	Lowcountry crab rice
	Joseph Buenconsejo	*Prospect Restaurant@ Scribner's Catskill Lodge*	Roasted chicken
	Nelly Buleje	*Metropolitan at The 9*	Branzino dish
	Ralph Burgin	*Sutro's at the Cliff House*	Sushi grade ahi tuna tartar
	David Burke	*Tavern62 by David Burke*	Lobster scramble
	Thomas Cardarelli	*Vermilion*	Heirloom tomato tart with garden herbs, tomato conserva and whipped ricotta
	Lysielle Cariot	*Bleu Provence*	Pan-sautéed cobia with coconut and cilantro red pepper sauce
	Jeff Chanchaleune	*Goro Ramen + Izakaya*	Soy braised pork belly
	Clayton Chapman	*The Grey Plume*	Whole roasted steelhead trout with creme fraiche, spatzle and seasonal vegetables
	Anthony Chittum	*Iron Gate Restaurant*	Cauliflower soup

Foodie fact #4

Fine dining was created in France. After the French Revolution, chefs that had worked for nobility were out of a job so they opened their own restaurants.

Michael Anthony - *Gramercy Tavern*
Roasted delicata squash with chicories, hazelnuts and pears
Unlock these 250 recipes on the free CHARITABLE BOOKINGS lifestyle app

RALPH BURGIN
Sutro's at the Cliff House

SUSHI GRADE AHI TUNA TARTAR
SERVES 4 | PREPARATION TIME 1 HOUR + 24 HOURS TO REST THE SAUCE

For the Sesame Oil
2 habaneros, coarsely chopped and handled using gloves
112g (*4 oz*) sesame oil

For the Dish
56g (*2 oz*) garlic, finely chopped
56g (*2 oz*) jalapeños, finely chopped and seeds removed
56g (*2 oz*) Asian pear, finely diced
56g (*2 oz*) red bell pepper, finely diced
56g (*2 oz*) pine nuts, chopped

8 leaves of mint, thinly sliced
225g (*8 oz*) sushi grade ahi tuna, diced
4 quail eggs, yolk only
sea salt
crackers or toast, to serve
Aleppo pepper

Start your preparation the day before by chopping the habaneros, placing in a small pot and adding sesame oil. Bring to a simmer, turn off heat and let it sit for a few hours to allow the flavours to comingle. Strain and keep in a squirt bottle at room temperature.

On the day of serving, an hour before you plate, prepare the garlic, jalapeños, Asian pear, bell pepper, pine nuts and mint. Place the diced tuna in a stainless steel mixing bowl and add sea salt plus 42ml (*1½ oz*) of infused sesame oil.

Just before serving, arrange the tuna tartar in the centre of the plate, with 56g (*2 oz*) per serving, using the ring mold. Make a small indentation on top of the tartar to hold the quail egg yolk. Arrange all of the garnishes decoratively around the tartar, as shown in the picture. Squeeze the sesame oil around it and sprinkle with Aleppo pepper and mint. Place the quail egg yolk on top of the tartar and serve immediately with crackers or toast.

ANTHONY CHITTUM
Iron Gate Restaurant

CAULIFLOWER SOUP
SERVES 4 | PREPARATION TIME 20 MINUTES | COOKING TIME 30 MINUTES

For the Dish
1 cauliflower
½ sweet onion, small
1 garlic, butt removed
568ml (*2 cups*) vegetable stock
946ml (*1 quart*) milk
4 tbsp cream

2 tsp capers
2 tsp golden raisins
1 tsp almonds, toasted
1 tsp parsley, chopped
2 tsp extra virgin olive oil
1 pinch curry powder
salt and pepper, to taste

To prepare the dish, remove the cauliflower florets from the stem, roughly chop and put in a medium soup pot. Peel the stems, roughly chop and add to the pot as well. Now roughly chop the onion and add to the pot along with the garlic, stock, milk and cream. Place the pot over a high heat and bring to a simmer and reduce the heat to low.

Simmer the soup until very tender. Purée the solids of the soup using only enough of the liquid to make desired consistency. Adjust the seasoning of the soup to desired level. Strain the soup back in the pot and keep it warm. Mix the capers, raisins, almonds, parsley, olive oil, curry powder and salt and pepper in a mixing bowl and set aside.

Split the soup between four bowls and place equal parts of the raisin mix in the center before serving.

	Sachin Chopra	*All Spice at San Mateo*	Lamb ragout à L'indien
	David Codney	*Belvedere at Peninsula Hotel*	Charred Caesar salad
	Tyson Cole	*Uchi*	Shima aji crudo
	Daniel Corey	*Luce*	Ravioli sweet bread
	Chris Cosentino	*Cockscomb*	Foie gras with pig's feet, strawberry jam and brioche
	Sllin Cruz	*Geronimo*	Mesquite grilled peppery elk tenderloin with garlic confit potatoes and exotic mushroom sauce
	Chris Cummer	*22 Square*	Swine and fowl with braised chicken and pork belly with strawberry jalapeño preserves
	Christophe De Lellis	*Joel Robuchon at The MGM Grand*	Sunchoke soup
	Martha De Leon	*Pax Americana*	Portuguese octopus in tomato paprika broth
	Mike DeCamp	*Monello*	Torchio braised rabbit, creme fraiche and artichokes

Foodie fact #5
The word "restaurant" was first used in English in 1806. Before that the term "eating-house" was used.

Jeff Balfour - *Southerleigh Fine Food & Brewery*
Braised oxtail sopes
Unlock these 250 recipes on the free CHARITABLE **BOOKINGS** lifestyle app.

CHRISTOPHE DE LELLIS
Joel Robuchon at The MGM Grand

SUNCHOKE SOUP
SERVES 4 | PREPARATION TIME 30 MINUTES | COOKING TIME 2 HOURS 30 MINUTES

For the Bouillon De Jambon
226g (*8 oz*) ham bones
113g (*4 oz*) ham meat
100g (*3½ oz*) ham fat
1.5l (*6.3 cups*) water
0.75l (*3.15*) cups chicken bouillon

For the Garlic Cream
56g (*2 oz*) garlic, degermed
56g (*2 oz*) heavy cream

For the Sunchoke Cream
250g (*8.8 oz*) sunchokes
42g (*1.5 oz*) onions
250g (*8.8 oz*) ham bouillon
250g (*8.8 oz*) heavy cream
34g (*1.2 oz*) butter

For the Parmesan Flan
107g (*3.8 oz*) milk
54g (*1.7 oz*) heavy cream
23g (*0.8 oz*) chicken bouillon
28g (*1 oz*) grated Parmesan
56g (*2 oz*) eggs
23g (*0.8 oz*) garlic cream
2g (*0.07 oz*) piment d'espelette

To prepare the dish, start with the bouillon de jambon. Blanch the bones, meat and fat in tap water. Bring to a boil and rinse in running water. Place all in rond d'eau with 1.5l (*6.3 cups*) of bottle water and the chicken bouillon. Bring to a boil. Simmer for 1 hour. Remove from the heat. Cover with plastic wrap and let rest. Strain in a chinois.

To make the garlic cream, blanch the garlic five times and blend with cream for 10 minutes. Season. Now make the sunchoke cream by peeling and finely slicing the sunchokes. Sweat in half of the butter for 25 minutes. Sweat the onions separately in the remaining butter. Add the bouillon to the onions and sunchoke. Simmer for 40 minutes. Blend. Add cream. Season and strain through a chinois.

Finish by making the Parmesan flan by heating the milk, blending boiling milk with Parmesan and adding the remaining ingredients. Blend for 10 minutes and strain through a chinois.

SYLVAIN DELPIQUE
21 Club

21 CLUB - STEAK TARTARE
SERVES 4 | PREPARATION TIME 30 MINUTES | COOKING TIME 5 HOURS

For the Dish
453g (*16 oz*) top quality filet mignon, we use prime, non-aged Black Angus beef
4 quail eggs
4 tbsp capers, chopped
4 tbsp cornichons, chopped
4 tbsp parsley, chopped
4 tbsp red onion, diced
2 tbsp extra virgin olive oil
sea salt and fresh ground pepper, to taste

For the Sauce
28g (*1 oz*) ketchup
28g (*1 oz*) Dijon mustard
28g (*1 oz*) Worcestershire sauce
1 tbsp Tabasco sauce

To prepare the dish, hand cut the beef into small cubes and keep refrigerated.

Combine all of the sauce ingredients and keep refrigerated.

Just before serving, take a large bowl and combine the beef, capers, cornichons, parsley and red onion. Season with sea salt and pepper. Add the sauce and extra virgin olive oil. Use a ring mold to plate the tartare and top each serving with a quail egg. Garnish with petit greens in truffle vinaigrette and shaved truffles. Serve with slice of toast.

	Sylvain Delpique	*21 Club*	21 Club steak tartare
	Dave DeVoss	*Cocothe*	Beef tartare
	Anthony Devoti	*Five Bistro*	35 minute roasted chicken
	Francesco Di Caudo	*Ferraro's Restaurant*	Braised short ribs
	Marc Djozlija	*Wright & Co*	Roasted pork tenderloin with goat cheese potato puree, pickled apricots, golden raisins and whole grain mustard sauce
	Matthew Dolan	*25 Lusk*	Fennel and grapefruit steamed manila clams with apple
	Shaun Doty	*The Federal*	Chicken schnitzel
	Joshua Drage	*Granite Lodge*	Buttermilk Tabasco chicken
	Alisha Elenz	*MFK Restaurant*	Seafood fideos with piperade and saffron-cream sauce
	Nicholas Elmer	*La Corte Bistro*	Pasta pescada

Foodie fact #6
The patron saint of cooks is
St. Martha.

Lidia Bastianich - *Lidia's*
Roasted loin of pork stuffed with prunes
Unlock these 250 recipes on the free CHARITABLE **BOOKINGS** lifestyle app.

SERGE FALCOZ-VIGNE
Saint Jacques French Cuisine

TERRINE LAPIN-RABBIT PÂTÉ
SERVES 8 | PREPARATION TIME 2 HOURS 30 MINUTES + 24 HOURS TO REST | COOKING TIME 15 MINUTES

Equipment
thermometer
For the Dish
1.35kg (3 lbs) pork, coarsely ground
1 rabbit, deboned, coarsely ground
2 tbsp brandy
1 cup celery, small dice

1 cup carrots, small dice
1 cup onions, small dice
60g (¼ cup) duck fat
32g (¼ cup) chopped garlic
2 tbsp fresh thyme, chopped
2 tbsp Kosher salt
2 tsp white pepper freshly ground
1 egg

To Serve
whole grain mustard
fresh baguette
cornichons
white wine

To prepare the dish, start by doing your shopping and finding a good local pork supplier. Then grind the pork coarsely. Now debone your rabbit and also grind coarsely. Marinate with brandy.

Take a cast iron pan and sauté the carrots, onions and celery with duck fat until caramelized and aromatic. Cut the heat, add the garlic, stir and wait 30 seconds. Then add the chopped thyme and wait another 30 seconds. You should smell the flavors rising to your nose.

Take a big bowl and mix the meat with the sautéed vegetables, egg, salt and pepper. Manually mixing is very important, mechanical tools will hurt the meat and reveal the tension between the pork and the rabbit. Put it in a terrine mold, cook it at 150°C (300°F) in a bain-marie until the terrine reaches an internal temperature of 74°C (165°F). Let cool a little, rest, put in the fridge for 2 hours and wrap to preserve the flavor. Let the terrine set for 24 hours.

Serve with whole grain mustard, cornichons, butter, fresh baguette and a good French white wine.

TODD GRAY
Equinox Restaurant

GRILLED ASPARAGUS ON FONDUED LEEKS with shaved cashew cheese
SERVES 6 | PREPARATION TIME 15 MINUTES | COOKING TIME 20 MINUTES

For the Dish
36 medium asparagus, peeled
2 tbsp extra virgin olive oil
6 leeks, halved and thinly sliced
56g (*2 oz*) margarine
2 tbsp extra virgin olive oil
472 ml (*16 fl oz*) vegetable broth
1 tsp fennel seeds, toasted and crushed
1 piece of cashew cheese
salt and peper

For the Truffle Vinaigrette
85ml (*2.9 fl oz*) balsamic vinegar
56ml (*1.9 fl oz*) sherry vinegar
1 tsp Dijon mustard
1 small black truffle, minced
½ tsp truffle oil
½ tsp canola oil
½ cup extra virgin olive oil
salt and pepper

For the dish. Heat a large, 7 litre (*6-quart*) sauté pan over a medium-low heat. Add margarine and olive oil and sauté the leeks until they are translucent. Season with the spices. Add the vegetable broth, cover and turn the heat to low. Allow the leeks to cook gently for 10 minutes until tender. Heat the grill to a high temperature and toss the asapargus in the additional 2 tbsp of olive oil, season and place onto the grill. Char until just tender, which will take approximately 2-3 minutes.

To prepare the truffle vinaigrette, combine all the ingredients and whisk vigorously to blend.

To serve, drain the leeks and place on the dishes. Cut the asparagus in half and place on top of the leeks. Drizzle with truffle vinaigrette. Garnish with shaved cashew cheese.

	Serge Falcoz-Vigne	*Saint Jacques French Cuisine*	Terrine lapin-rabbit pâté
	Kathy Fang	*Fang*	Kung pao salmon with sweet potato and brocolli
	Enzo Febbraro	*Allegro*	Lasagna with Sunday ragu sauce
	Gavin Fine	*The Kitchen*	Seared sea scallops with Asian vin
	Dan Fisher	*Society Fair*	Spanish seafood stew
	Jay Flatley	*Tavern*	Mexican street tots
	Marc Forgione	*Marc Forgione*	Chili lobster
	Janine Fourie	*Big Easy*	Slow roasted lamb shank bunny
	Raphael Francois	*Le DeSales*	Crabe simplissime
	Jacky Francois	*The Main Dining Room at Omni Mount Washington Resort*	Seafood tower with a spicy mango gazpacho sauce

Foodie fact #7
Ketchup was sold in the
1830's as medicine.

Emma Bengtsson - Aquavit
Sirloin and cabbage
Unlock these 250 recipes on the free CHARITABLE BOOKINGS lifestyle app.

TROY GUARD
Guard and Grace

PAN SEARED ALAMOSA STRIPED BASS

SERVES 4 | PREPARATION TIME 10 MINUTES | COOKING TIME 15 MINUTES

For the Dish
140g (*5oz*) Alamosa striped
bass filet, skin on, pin bones
removed
57g (*2oz*) grapeseed oil
Kosher salt, to sprinkle
1 tbsp celery leaves, chopped
36g (*¼ cup*) Hawaiian Hearts
of Palm

For the Lentils
200g (*1 cup*) black lentils
720g (*3 cups*) stock, broth or
water
4 tbsp onion, small dice, charred
4 tbsp carrot, small dice, charred
4 tbsp soy beans
57g (*2oz*) king crab
57g (*2oz*) brown butter
1 tbsp chives, small cut

For the Sauce
120g (*½ cup*) blood orange juice
85g (*¼ cup*) honey vinegar
60g (*¼ cup*) olive oil

To prepare the dish, start by cooking the lentils. In a medium saucepan, add the lentils and 3 cups of cooking liquid; bring to a boil. Reduce heat and simmer, partially covered, until lentils are soft, 30-40 minutes. Set aside. Heat the sauté pan and add 57g (*2 oz*) grapeseed oil. Season the skin side with Kosher salt, then hard sear skin side down on a medium high heat. When it starts to get a golden brown crust, turn off the gas finish in the pan to medium doneness (*3-5 minutes*). The skin should be crisp. Remove the fish from the pan, then mix all the lentil ingredients together in the same pan to utilize the fish drippings and hot pan. The lentil mix should be warm, not hot.

Place the lentil mix in a ring mold and place in the middle of a plate. Place the fish on top of the lentils. In the same sauté pan, reduce the blood orange juice and vinegar down by half, then place in blender. While blending, slowly drizzle oil in to emulsify.

To finish, drizzle the blood orange sauce around the plate and garnish with celery leaves and hearts of palm.

FRANCIS HOGAN
Sabio on Main

VIETNAMESE STEAK TARTARE
SERVES 4 | PREPARATION TIME 1 HOUR | COOKING TIME 10 MINUTES

Equipment
candy thermometer

For the Dish
2l (*2 quarts*) rice bran or other high quality frying oil
1 pack uncooked shrimp chips prawn crackers
340g (*12 oz*) high quality, beef tenderloin, trimmed

120g (*4 cups*) mixed fresh herbs and flowers - mint, pea shoots, coriander blossom, nasturtium, Thai basil, radish pods, mustard flowers, picked and washed
2 tbsp high quality fish sauce
1½ tbsp rice wine vinegar
2 tbsp lime juice
2 tbsp brown sugar

1 garlic clove, minced
½ inch peeled ginger, grated
½ fresno chili, minced
4 quail eggs
1 tbsp shallots, minced
1 tsp garlic, chopped, fried
2 tsp toasted rice flour
scant flaked sea salt

To prepare the dish, take a large stock pot and heat the 2l (*2 quarts*) of oil to 190°C (*375°F*), using the candy thermometer to monitor. Once the oil is hot, start adding shrimp chips, making sure not to over crowd the pot. When the chips have puffed, remove from the oil and drain on a napkin lined sheet. Repeat with remaining chips. Now make the nuoc cham. Combine the fish sauce, vinegar, lime, brown sugar, garlic, ginger, and chili in a small bowl. Mix well and allow to sit for 30 minutes. Fill a bowl with ice and place another bowl inside to stay cold. Dice the beef and move it to the chilled bowl. Add the nuoc cham, shallots, rice flour and garlic to the beef and mix very well. Let the beef rest for 5 minutes to meld the flavors. Taste for seasoning. It should be well seasoned, but slightly under salted. Gather the herb mixture and quail eggs and proceed to plating.

To finish and serve, place the ring mold in the center of a salad plate. Using a spoon, pack the beef into the mold as tight as possible, but don't squeeze out too much dressing. Carefully remove the ring mold to keep the beef in its shape. Use the herb salad to form a wreath completely encircling the beef mold. Make a divot in the center of the beef. Carefully cut the top of the quail egg shell clean off. Remove the quail egg from the shell; separate the yolk from the white. Return the yolk to its shell and place the shell, cut side up into the divot in the beef. Lightly sprinkle the sea salt on the dish to taste, paying most attention to the beef. Serve immediately with shrimp chips and sambal oleck on the side.

	Neal Fraser	*Redbird*	Lamb belly with jerk spice with pineapple and cabbage pancake
	Tom French	*Joshua Wilton House*	Beef short rib pasta
	Devin Gainor	*Azure Openfront Restaurant at the Shores Resort & Spa*	Cilantro seared diver scallops with roasted poblano and avocado hash
	Michael Galen	*Dusek's Board & Beer*	Chicken fried rabbit recipe
	Jonathan Garcia	*El Gaucho*	Braised lamb shank with saffron risotto
	Kevin Gillespie	*Revival*	Coca-Cola braised pot roast
	Michael Glatz	*Hotel Fauchere*	Sushi pizza
	Markus Glocker	*Batard*	Octopus pastrami with hamhock
	Todd Gray	*Equinox Restaurant*	Grilled asparagus on fondued leeks with shaved cashew cheese
	Christopher Gross	*Geordie's at the Wrigley Mansion*	Chicken roasted with portabellas

Foodie fact #8
The first avocado tree in the U.S.A.
was planted in Florida in 1833

Aaron Bludorn - *Cafe Boulud*
Stripped bass "en paupiette"
Unlock these 250 recipes on the free CHARITABLE BOOKINGS lifestyle app.

JONATHAN INSETTA

Black Sheep Restaurant Group

PEANUT BUTTER AND JELLY FOIE GRAS

SERVES 01-Apr | PREPARATION TIME 1 HOUR | COOKING TIME 1 HOUR

For the Dish
80g (2.8 oz) foie gras

For the Red Onion Marmalade
1kg (1 quart) red onion, brunoise
360ml (1½ cups) red wine vinegar
200g (1½ cup) sugar
1 tsp Kosher salt
1 sprig of thyme

For the Red Beet Fluid Gel
400ml (14 oz) red beet juice
100ml (3.5 oz) balsamic vinegar
5ml (0.2 oz) agar
5g (0.2 oz) Kosher salt,
0.5g (0.02 oz) xanthum gum

For the Custard Bread
1kg (32 oz) French baguette
6 (¾ cup) egg yolk
3 tbsp sugar
2 tsp salt
1kg (3 cups) 40% heavy cream

To prepare the dish, start by preparing the foie gras. Score and season lightly with salt and pepper. Sear the score side down until golden brown. Transfer to a baking sheet and put in a 120°C (225°F) oven for 5 minutes. For the red onion marmalade, combine the onions, vinegar, sugar, and salt into a medium sauté pan. Cook over a medium heat until thickened and the onions are translucent. Stir in thyme. Transfer marmalade to a sheet pan to cool in the refrigerator. Now make the red beet fluid gel by mixing the dry ingredients with a whisk. Transfer dry mix into a bowl with the beet juice. Set up an ice bath to the side. Place beet liquid into a sauce pan over medium heat and bring to a boil. Transfer liquid a bowl and place into the ice bath whisking until the liquid is chilled. Process the chilled liquid in a blender until smooth.

Now make the custard bread by mixing the yolk, sugar, salt and cream in a bowl. Pour over cubed baguettes and soak for 10 minutes. Spray loaf pan with pan spray. Bake at 175°C (350°F) for 25 minutes. Cool for 10 minutes before removing from pan.

To finish and serve, take a plate and swoosh the red beet fluid gel. Take warm custard bread and cut into a cube. Spread red onion marmalade on top. Place pan seared foie gras on top, like an open faced sandwich.

JOJI IOUNE
CHAYA Venice

UNI ICE CREAM
SERVES 5 | PREPARATION TIME 30 MINUTES | COOKING TIME 30 MINUTES

Equipment
ice cream maker
For the Dish
100g (*3.5 oz*) sea urchin
500ml (*17 fl oz*) soy cream

300ml (*10 fl oz*) soy milk
150g (*5 oz*) sugar
6 egg yolk
pinch of salt
10 pairs Japanese monaka

For the Tamari Port Wine Sauce
250ml (*8.5 fl oz*) ruby port wine
10ml (*0.4 fl oz*) tamari soy sauce

Start by making the uni ice cream. Combine the soy milk, sea urchin, and salt in a medium sauce pan. Heat over a medium heat, stirring frequently until bubbles form around the edges of the pan. Meanwhile, in a blender, process the sugar and egg yolks together until very thick and smooth. With the blender running, gradually add the soy cream. Return the mixture to the saucepan and cook over medium heat, stirring constantly with a wooden spoon, for 6 to 8 minutes. The custard is ready when it reaches 80°C (*176°F*) and coats the back of the spoon. Remove the pan from the heat and set it in a bowl of ice water. Stir the mixture briskly over the ice bath until chilled. In a deep bowl, beat the soy cream until it forms soft peaks. Remove the pan with the cooled custard mixture from the ice bath and gently fold in the whipped soy cream. Transfer to an ice cream maker and freeze.

Now make the Tamari port wine sauce by placing the port wine in a heavy bottomed saucepan over a medium high heat. Simmer uncovered until thickened and syrupy and reduced to 125ml (*4.4 fl oz*), which will take approximately 15-20 min. Remove from the heat and cool to room temperature. Whisk in tamari. Set aside.

To finish, place a dab of port sauce onto each of the 10 wafers and sprinkle lightly with sea salt. Put a scoop of the uni ice cream on top of the salt layer and gently press to flatten slightly. Top each sandwich with a second wafer.

	Ben Grupe	*ELAIA*	Carrot wrapped trout loin
	Troy Guard	*Guard and Grace*	Pan seared alamosa striped bass
	Jason Halverson	*Trestle*	Garganelli Bolognese
	Bobby Hansen	*Tartufo*	Meatballs in arrabiata sauce
	Nicholas Harary	*Restaurant Nicholas*	Coconut pumpkin soup
	Tim Hardiman	*The Tailor and the Cook*	Braised veal brisket
	Harvey Harris	*Siena Restaurant*	Bistecca Fiorentina
	Matthew Harris	*Tupelo Park City*	Fire roasted cauliflower with pork jowls with golden raisins and miso dressing
	Skip Hause	*Gertrude's*	Pear chile enchilada sauce
	Thomas Henkelmann	*Homestead Inn- Thomas Henkelmann*	Salmon in brick with Russian Ossetra caviar and sauce diable

James Boyce - *Cotton Row*
Braised beef short rib in red wine and pomegranate
Unlock these 250 recipes on the free CHARITABLE BOOKINGS lifestyle app

JEAN JOHO
Everest

SOLE PETITE GRENOBLOISE
SERVES 2 | PREPARATION TIME 20 MINUTES | COOKING TIME 20 MINUTES

For the Dish
240ml (*1 cup*) whole milk
60g (*½ cup*) Wondra flour
2 tbsp olive oil
2 Dover sole filets, trimmed and skinned
salt and freshly ground white pepper

1 tbsp unsalted butter
3 tbsp capers
½ lemon, juice of
1 tbsp flat-leaf parsley, minced
1 tbsp extra small croutons

To prepare the dish, pour the milk into a shallow container, like a baking dish, that is large enough to hold the fish. Put the flour in another shallow container. In a large skillet, heat the oil over medium-high heat until shimmering. Meanwhile coat a fish fillet on both sides in the milk, remove and season with salt and white pepper. Dredge the fillet in the flour, tapping off the excess flour. Repeat with the remaining fillets. Add the fillets to the pan and sauté until browned, about 3 minutes each side.

Transfer each fillet to a warmed serving plate. Wipe the pan clean and place over medium heat. Add the butter and cook until melted and starting to brown , about 1 minute. Stir in the capers. Remove the pan from the heat and stir in the lemon juice.

Spoon the sauce over the sole, garnish with the parsley and croutons, and serve at once.

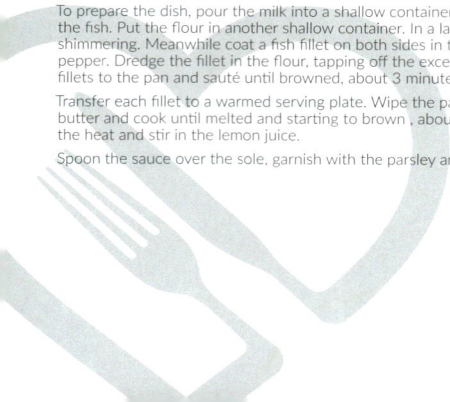

DAVE JONES
Log Haven

GRILLED OCTOPUS AND CALAMARI
SERVES 4 | PREPARATION TIME 15 MINUTES | COOKING TIME 5 MINUTES

For the Dish
450g (*1 lb*) calamari, cleaned
450g (*1 lb*) prepared octopus, sliced
3 tbsp extra virgin olive oil
1 lemon, juiced
1 tbsp parsley, chopped
salt and chile flakes
capers, to garnish
lemon aioli, to garnish
chive oil, to garnish
shaved Parmesan, to garnish

For the Black Olive Pesto
200g (*2½ cups*) whole cerignola olives
5 cloves garlic
½ zested lemon
½ juiced lemon
85ml (*⅜ cup*) extra virgin olive oil
1 tsp red chile flakes
3 tbsp pine nuts
42g (*¼ cup*) grated Grana Padano
1 tsp parsley, chopped
salt, to taste

For the Eggplant Tomato Coulis
5 peeled, seeded and chopped Roma tomatoes
1 cup eggplant, grilled, diced
1-2 shallots, fine dice
3 cloves garlic, chopped
1 lemon, juiced
3-4 tbsp extra virgin olive oil
1 tbsp Italian parsley, chopped
salt and Aleppo pepper, to taste

This is a remarkably simple dish to make that emphasis the beauty of fresh, flavorsome ingredients. Start the dish by taking the calamari and octopus and grilling for two minutes until done, dressing with the olive oil, lemon, chopped parsley, salt and chile flakes.

Make the black olive pesto by blending the ingredients together, except the salt. Taste. Since the olives contain so much salt, you may or may not want to add further salt. Now make the eggplant tomato cous cous by mixing the prepared ingredients together.

Garnish with capers, lemon aioli, chive oil and shaved Parmesan.

	Caleb Higginson	*Sophia's*	Clam cake
	Gerald Hirigoyen	*Piperade*	Oxtails braised in red wine
	Francis Hogan	*Sabio on Main*	Vietnamese steak tartare
	Zane Holmquist	*The Glitretind Restaurant at Stein Eriksen Lodge*	Wild game chilli
	John Howie	*Seastar Restaurant & Raw Bar*	Steamed clams with pesto
	Jonathan Insetta	*Black Sheep Restaurant Group*	Peanut butter and jelly foie gras
	Joji Ioune	*CHAYA Venice*	Uni ice cream
	Pat Jeung	*Chameleon Restaurant & Bar*	Salmon curry
	Jean Joho	*Everest*	Sole petite grenobloise
	Dave Jones	*Log Haven*	Grilled octopus and calamari

Foodie fact #10

Apple Pie is not an American creation. Pies were first created in medieval England while the apple pie with the lattice crust we know today is from a Dutch recipe.

David Burke – *Tavern62 by David Burke*
Lobster scramble

Unlock these 250 recipes on the free CHARITABLE **BOOKINGS** lifestyle app.

BRADLEY KILGORE
Alter

SOFT EGG
SERVES 2 | PREPARATION TIME 30 MINUTES | COOKING TIME 30 MINUTES

Equipment
VitaMix blender
ISI charger and cartridges
For the Dish
1.3kg (*46 oz*) cream
3 bay leaves
2.5g (*0.09 oz*) thyme
2.5g (*0.09 oz*) rosemary

125g (*4.4 oz*) shallot
10g (*0.35 oz*) garlic
300g (*11 oz*) sea scallop
225g (*8 oz*) gruyère
40ml (*1.4 oz*) lemon juice
13ml (*0.46 oz*) truffle oil
salt
1g (*0.04 oz*) xantham

For the Garnish
olive oil
black truffle oil
chives, thinly sliced
sea salt
chive flowers

To make the dish, start with the sea scallop espuma. Bring the first set of ingredients up to a simmer with the cream and cook for 5 minutes. Strain through chinois into the VitaMix pitcher. On high heat blend in the scallops and the cheese a little at a time. Follow with the xantham gum and use the plunger if necessary.

Finish with the rest of the ingredients and pass through a chinois. Immediately charge in the ISI with two charges. Hold at 50°C (*120°F*) until needed. Now make the gruyère crisps by cooking grated gruyère in the oven at 150°C (*300°F*) until dry and crispy but with no color. Dry and store in a dry container.

Garnish and plate as pictured.

RICHARD LAUGHLIN

Salt at The Ritz Carlton - Amelia Island

BUTTERNUT SQUASH SOUP

SERVES 8-10 | PREPARATION TIME 1 HOUR | COOKING TIME 1 HOUR 30 MINUTES

For the Dish
3 large butternut squash
284ml (*1 cup*) apple juice
568ml (*2 cups*) heavy cream
1l (*3 cups*) whole milk
½ tsp nutmeg, ground
½ tsp cloves, ground
½ tsp allspice, ground
113g (*½ cup*) unsalted butter
Kosher salt to taste

To prepare the dish, cut the squash in half and remove seeds. On a sheet pan bake squash skin side up at 176°C (350°F) for 40-50 minutes or until soft.

After squash is cooked and cooling, add all remaining ingredients into a large pot and bring to a simmer. When the ingredients are simmering, take off the heat.

Now scoop the pulp out of the squash and add pulp to the liquid. Stir well and bring back to a simmer then turn off. In small batches, add soup to a blender and purée until smooth.

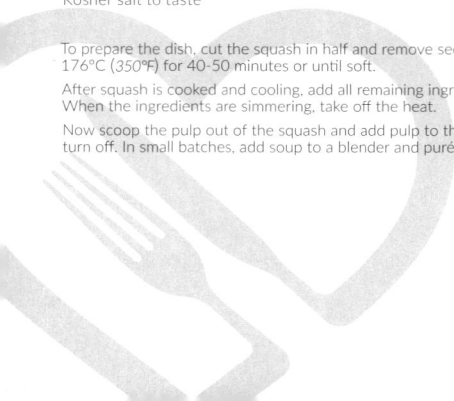

	Nic Jones	*Goose and Gander*	Roasted chicken breast with white truffle gravy
	Douglas Katz	*Fire Food and Drink*	Harissa roasted chicken thighs with moroccan cous cous
	Matthew Kenney	*Plant*	Black pepper kelp noodles with sunflower cream, spicy greens, green olive puree and sundried olives
	Brandon Kida	*Hinoki & The bird*	California black cod
	Bradley Kilgore	*Alter*	Soft egg
	James Kim	*Morandi*	Gnocchi with porcini and chestnut
	David Kinch	*Manresa*	Into the vegetable garden
	Michael Kloeti	*Michael's on the Hill*	Wild mushroom soup with ramp pistou
	Jason Knibb	*Nine-Ten*	Jamaican jerk pork belly with black eyed peas, garnet yam purée and scotch bonnet pepper jellies
	Gabriel Kreuther	*Gabriel Kreuther*	Sturgeon and sauerkraut tart topped with American sturgeon caviar

Foodie fact #11
In 18th century Europe the tomato was known as the "poison apple"
and was considered to be deadly.

Chris Cummer - *22 Square*
Swine and fowl with braised chicken and pork belly with strawberry jalapeño preserves
Unlock these 250 recipes on the free CHARITABLE BOOKINGS lifestyle app.

JUN LEE
River Yacht Club

SALMON CRUDO
SERVES 4 | PREPARATION TIME 4 HOURS

Equipment
Vitamix
For the Salmon
236ml (*1 cup*) red beet juice
1 orange
5g (*0.18 oz*) parsley
2 sticks of thyme

For the Orange Soy Dressing
100ml (*4.7 fl oz*) orange juice syrup
1 tsp pepper flakes
40ml (*1.9 fl oz*) lemon juice
40ml (*1.9 fl oz*) lime juice
40ml (*1.9 fl oz*) yuzu juice
80ml (*3.8 fl oz*) soy sauce
40g (*1.9 fl oz*) honey
40ml (*1.9 fl oz*) olive oil
1 lime, zested
1 lemon, zested
10g (*0.35 oz*) ginger

For the Horseradish Cream
200g (*9.4 fl oz*) heavy cream
20g (*0.7 oz*) horseradish
salt
For the Garnish
10 cherry radish slices
10 pearl onion slices
10 pieces of micro cilantro
Shredded seaweed

To marinate the salmon, place in with the beet juice, parsley and orange zest for at least three hours. Wash and dry all of the beet juice then slice the salmon to about an inch. Cover and very tightly wrap before storing in the fridge until ready to use.

To prepare the orange soy dressing combine orange syrup, lemon juice, lime juice, yuzu juice, soy sauce, honey and pepper flakes in a Vitamix, slowly blend. Add the olive oil and ginger, keep blending until well mixed. Place the mixture in a large bowl and add the lime and lemon zest. Mix with a whisk. Place in the squeezy bottles and store in the fridge.

To prepare the horseradish cream, beat the cream until it forms firm peaks. Add the horseradish and salt. Whisk very gently until well mixed. Place in a squeezy bottle and store in the fridge.

To serve, roll the salmon and place the rolls on the plate. Each piece of salmon should be about a tenth of an inch thick and there should be 10 pieces per order. Drizzle the orange soy dressing on top and add any excess to the plate. Add five dots of horseradish cream. Evenly add the sliced radish, sliced onion and micro cilantro. Finish with the shredded seaweed.

NATE LINDSAY
Lucy Restaurant and Bar at Bardessono

LUCY GARDEN CRUDITÉ

SERVES 4 | PREPARATION TIME 1 HOUR 30 MINUTES | COOKING TIME 1 HOUR

Equipment
mandoline

For the Dish
320g (*2 cups*) fresh green chickpeas, shelled, blanched and shocked
3 cloves of garlic
½ lemon, juiced
1 tbsp ground cumin
55ml (*¼ cup*) grapeseed oil
2 tbsp cilantro, chopped
½ tsp Kosher salt
½ English cucumber, sliced
¼ head cauliflower, florets removed from stem
10 pole beans, blanched and shocked
12 cherry tomatoes, halved
6 English peas, split in half with the peas remaining
2 each squash, zucchini and Easter radish, sliced lengthwise ¼ inch on mandoline
1 heirloom tomato, grated on box grater
1 tbsp sherry vinegar
1 tsp Dijon mustard
1 tsp honey
55ml (*¼ cup*) grapeseed oil

To prepare the dish, start with the chickpea hummus by placing the chickpeas into boiling water for 2 minutes, then place in ice water. Strain the chickpeas and place them into the food processor. Add the garlic, lemon juice, cumin, oil, salt and pepper. Blend until smooth but not runny. Fold in cilantro and adjust seasoning if needed. Now make the tomato vinaigrette by placing the grated tomato, vinegar, mustard and honey into the food processor. Turn on and blend while adding a slow stream of oil into the mixture. Season with salt and pepper as needed.

To prepare the zucchini and squash rolls, place the seasoned squash on a greased sheet pan. Bake for 4 minutes at 176°C (*350°F*). Once cool to the touch, roll them up. Using a ring mold, place the hummus in the center and smooth out to the edges. Remove the ring mold from the hummus. Place all the seasoned vegetables throughout the surface of the hummus. Add some vinaigrette to the plate next to the crudité. Finish the vegetables with extra virgin olive oil, sea salt and cracked black pepper.

	David Ladner	*Sandbar*	Roasted cauliflower caponata with salsa verde
	Emeril Lagasse	*Emeril's Delmonico*	Emeril's Delmonico crispy pork cheeks with creole dirty rice
	Richard Landau	*Vedge*	Royal trumpet mushroom cioppino
	David Landrigan	*Circa 1875*	Pan seared loupe de mer sea bass
	Tim Lanza	*Marigold Kitchen*	Pan seared cervena venison
	Richard Laughlin	*Salt at The Ritz Carlton - Amelia Island*	Butternut squash soup
	Jun Lee	*River Yacht Club*	Salmon crudo
	Joshua Lewin	*Juliet*	Salt roasted branzino with fennel scalloped potatoes
	Enrique Limardo	*Alma Cocina Latina*	Fried chicken with apples
	Nate Lindsay	*Lucy Restaurant and Bar at Bardessono*	Lucy garden crudite

Foodie fact #12

The cheeseburger was created at the Humpty Dumpty Barrel restaurant in Colorado and trade-marked in 1935 by Louis E. Ballast.

Mike DeCamp - *Monello*
Torchio braised rabbit, creme fraiche and artichokes
Unlock these 250 recipes on the free CHARITABLE **BOOKINGS** lifestyle app.

VICTORIANO LOPEZ
La Mar

CEVICHE CLASICO
SERVES 4 | PREPARATION TIME 30 MINUTES

For the Leche De Tigre
6 - 8 key limes, freshly juiced
200g (*7 oz*) halibut filet
1 clove of garlic
900ml (*12 oz*) fish stock
½ habanero chili
1 sprig of cilantro
1 celery stalk
1 cup ice
1 medium white onion
salt, to taste

For the Ceviche Clasico
800g (*28 oz*) fresh California Halibut fillet
½ habanero chili, finely diced
28g (*1 oz*) each cooked yam, Peruvian corn and red onion, julienne
1 sprig of cilantro

To prepare the Leche de Tigre, blend all of the ingredients in a blender, strain the juice and set aside.

To prepare the ceviche clasico, chop the halibut into cubes, approximately 1 inch each, and place in a bowl. Add salt, habanero chili and ice cubes. Add the tiger's milk and stir. Let the mixture set for 30 seconds and then remove the ice cubes. Add the onion.

To serve, place the ceviche on a plate and garnish with onion, corn, cilantro and yams.

MARC LORUSSO
Costa Di Mare at The Wynn Hotel

SEARED SEA SCALLOPS
SERVES 4 | PREPARATION TIME 30 MINUTES | COOKING TIME 5 MINUTES

For the Dish
12 fresh sea scallops
2 tbsp olive oil
salt
1 cup fennel purée
570ml (*2 cups*) blood orange,
2 tbsp pistachio, lightly toasted

For the Blood Orange Vinaigrette
56ml (*2oz*) blood orange juice
170ml (*6oz*) olive oil
Kosher salt and black pepper
1 small shallot, finely minced

For the Fennel Purée
2 bulbs fennel, reserve the fronds
2 tbsp extra virgin olive oil
Kosher salt and black pepper

To prepare the dish, preheat an oven to 148°C (*300°F*). Place the pistachio nuts on a sheet pan and roast lightly for 10 minutes until warm and fragrant.

To make the blood orange vinaigrette, into a stainless steel bowl, mix the blood orange juice, olive oil, salt, pepper and shallot.

To make the fennel purée, split the fennel into quarters and remove core. Place the fennel in a small saucepan and cover with water. Boil over a high heat until the fennel is tender, which takes approximately 20 minutes. Drain the liquid. Place the fennel in a food processor fitted with a steel blade, add the olive oil and purée until smooth. Season with salt and pepper.

To finish the dish, pat the scallops dry with a paper towel and season with salt and pepper. Heat the oil in a large sauté pan over a medium heat and add the the scallops. Sauté without moving them for approximately three minutes on each side, until golden brown. Spread the warm fennel purée across a large platter; place the scallops over the fennel purée. Add the reserved blood orange segments to the vinaigrette and drizzle over and around the scallops. Garnish with the toasted pistachios and fennel fronds.

	Michele Lisi	*Nerano*	Ora king salmon
	Victoriano Lopez	*La Mar*	Ceviche Clasico
	Marc LoRusso	*Costa Di Mare at The Wynn Hotel*	Seared sea scallops
	Travis Maier	*Jeff Ruby's Steakhouse*	Seared Ohio trout
	Damian Mandola	*Carrabba's Italian Grill*	Mamma's whole roasted fish
	Laurent Manrique	*Cafe de la Presse*	Parnsip and pear soup with bay scallops
	Salvatore Marcello	*Mamo*	Capelli d'angelo with gambrel e pistachio
	Jose Martinez	*Maison Blanche*	Sauteed of wild shrimp with asparagus
	Justin Mason	*The Sun dial*	Pan-seared scallops
	Gabriel Massip	*Capa*	Hamachi crudo with eggplant and foie gras emulsion

Foodie fact #13
Ketchup was originally a fish sauce first recorded in the Malay language as "kitchap" from the Chinese "koechiap" meaning "brine of fish".

Jason Knibb - *Nine-Ten*
Jamaican jerk pork belly with black eyed peas, garnet yam puree and scotch bonnet pepper jellies

Unlock these 250 recipes on the free CHARITABLE BOOKINGS lifestyle app.

JAY MENDOZA
Azurea at One Ocean

CITRUS MARINATED PRAWNS
SERVES 4 | PREPARATION TIME 30 MINUTES + 4 HOURS TO MARINATE | COOKING TIME 25 MINUTES

For the Citrus Marinade
1 fresh orange, zested and juiced
1 lemon, zested and juiced
60ml (¼ cup) extra virgin olive oil
1 tsp fresh dill, chopped
1 tsp fresh thyme, chopped
1 tsp fresh rosemary, chopped
16 prawns

For the Corn and Spring Peas Succotash
60ml (¼ cup) olive oil
40g (¼ cup) red onion, small diced
2 garlic cloves, thinly sliced
40g (¼ cup) cherry tomatoes, halved
165g (1 cup) corn

75g (½ cup) spring peas
1 tsp fresh paprika
1 tsp thyme, chopped
1 tsp tarragon, chopped
1 cup vegetable stock
¼ stick of butter
salt and pepper, to taste

To make the dish, create the citrus marinade by taking a small bowl and adding the prawns with all of the other ingredients and fresh herbs. Marinate for at least 4 hours before grilling.

Take a large sauté pan and place over a very low heat. Add the olive oil. Add the red onions and sweat till translucent, Add the corn kernels and spring peas and toss. Add the garlic and stir thoroughly to prevent burning. Add the fresh herbs and cook for about 1 minute. Slowly add the vegetable stock and reduced in half. Combine the fresh cherry tomatoes. Slowly add the butter and tossed continuously. Season with salt and pepper.

To grill the shrimp, turn the grill to a high heat. Slowly add the shrimp and season with salt and pepper. Cook the shrimp for about 1minute to 2 minutes on each side until it has a little char on the outside and is cooked inside, being careful not to burn. Drizzle with a little bit of olive oil and fresh chopped herbs. Set aside for plating. Plate by arranging the corn and spring pea succotash in the center of the plate. Add 4 shrimp down the middle. Garnish with pea sprouts, or any edible flowers and drizzle the plate with balsamic vinegar and olive oil and finish off with sea salt and fresh cracked pepper.

ALEJANDRO MORGAN
Lolinda

CEVICHE DE PESCADO
SERVES 4 | PREPARATION TIME 10 MINUTES

For the Dish
450g (*1 lb*) white fish filet, local halibut or ono
¼ red onion, thinly sliced
1 tbsp cilantro, chopped
1 habanero, chopped, optional
1 lime, juiced
1 yam boiled until soft, cut into bite-sized pieces
350ml (*1½ cups*) leche de tigre

For the Leche De Tigre
720ml (*3 cups*) lime juice
3 cups ice
60g (*½ cup*) celery, chopped
3 cloves garlic
1 tbsp ginger, diced
60g (*½ cup*) red onion hearts
½ tbsp salt
2 tbsp sugar
5 sprigs cilantro
100g (*½ cup*) rocoto pepper paste

aji amarillo, to taste

To prepare the dish, start by working with the fish. Slice the fish into 1/4 inch thick pieces and put in a mixing bowl. Add the cilantro, red onion, habanero, lime juice, and season with a couple pinches of salt.

To make the leche de tigre, put the lime juice, ice, celery, garlic, ginger, sugar, and salt in a blender and blend until all ingredients are incorporated. Add the onion and cilantro to the blender and pulse for 2 seconds, just to get some flavor out. Be careful not to blend more than a couple of seconds because the sauce will turn bitter. Strain liquid in a chinoise. Add the aji amarillo or rocotto pepper paste.

Add the leche de tigre to the fish. Let it sit in the sauce for no more than one minute. Serve over yams and corn.

	Carl McConnell	*Stone Soup Cottage*	Smoked duck cannelloni with brown butter and lavender
	Shaun McCrain	*Copine Seattle*	White beans and clams
	Jen McMahon	*Da Flora*	Pan seared dayboat scallops with sugar pie pumpkin purée, crisped jen of the woods mushrooms, balsamic brown butter glaze
	Kevin Meehan	*Kali*	Charred avocado salad
	Justin Melnick	*The Terrace at the Charlotte Inn*	Lobster duo
	Jay Mendoza	*Azurea at One Ocean*	Citrus marinated prawns
	Ouita Michel	*Holly Hill Inn*	Happy Jack's sweet corn salad
	Christophe Mihy	*El Chorro Lodge*	Signature beef strogonoff
	Harry Mills	*Purple Cafe and Wine Bar*	Spanish clams
	Kasey Mills	*Mediterranean Exploration Company/ Ya'all*	Moroccan chicken

Foodie fact #14
Hawaii is the only US State to
grow coffee beans.

Gabriel Kreuther - *Gabriel Kreuther*
Sturgeon and sauerkraut tart topped with American sturgeon caviar
Unlock these 250 recipes on the free CHARITABLE BOOKINGS lifestyle app.

BRIAN MURPHY
Nostrana

VONGOLE BIANCO PIZZA
SERVES 02-APR | PREPARATION TIME 30 MINUTES | COOKING TIME 8-10 MINUTES

Equipment
pizza stone or baking sheet
pizza peel or baking sheet

For the Dish
226g (½lb) homemade or store-bought pizza dough, enough for one 10-12inch pizza
½ tsp oregano, fresh minced
1 tbsp extra virgin olive oil
1 clove garlic, thinly sliced
2 tbsp provolone picante, shredded
2 tbsp smoked mozzarella cheese, shredded
2 tbsp peppadew peppers, finely chopped
10 Manila clams, washed
1 tbsp gremolata, see recipe below
juice from a quarter lemon

For the Gremolata
6g (¼ cup) parsley, finely chopped
¼ clove garlic
grated zest of 1 lemon

To prepare the dish, preheat the oven to its highest temperature at 260°C (500°F) or higher. If you have a pizza stone, place it on the middle rack of the oven and allow it to preheat for at least 30 minutes. Form dough into 10-12inch pizza base. Sprinkle a handful of flour on a pizza peel or the back of a baking sheet. Form dough into a large disk with your hands and lay it on the peel. Using your hands or a rolling pin, flatten the dough until it is 1/4inch thick or less. Shake the peel or baking sheet frequently as you shape to ensure the dough isn't sticking. Use additional flour if dough sticks. If the dough starts to shrink back, let it rest for 5 minutes and then continue rolling until 10-12inches. Sprinkle dough with oregano, spread garlic on base of pie and drizzle with olive oil, evenly. Sprinkle provolone and smoked mozzarella cheese over base of pie, then spread finely chopped peppadew peppers evenly. Place 10 small manila clams evenly over pizza, more or less, depending on size.

Bake your pizza. Using a pizza peel or the back side of a baking sheet, slide your pizza onto the pre-heated baking stone and cook for 5 minutes. Rotate the pizza and cook for an additional 3-5 minutes, or until edges are browned and crispy and manila clams "pop" open. Make the gremolata by mixing together all of the ingredients in a mixing bowl. Store in an airtight container. Remove from oven and finish with a generous teaspoon of gremolata and the juice of a quarter lemon.

FERNANDO NAVAS

Kingside at The Viceroy Hotel

CIOPPINO

SERVES 4 | PREPARATION TIME 3 HOURS | COOKING TIME 1 HOUR

For the Dish
170g (*6 oz*) Spanish onion, small dice
170g (*6 oz*) tomato, skin off, small dice
85g (*3 oz*) fennel, thinly sliced
3 cloves garlic, thinly sliced
60ml (*2 fl oz*) extra virgin olive oil
85g (*3 oz*) chorizo, small dice
2 bay leaves
120ml (*4 fl oz*) dry white wine
473ml (*16 fl oz*) shrimp stock

3 saffron threads
white pepper, to taste
4 x 113g (*4 oz*) striped bass filets
8 mussels
8 Middle Neck clams
113g (*4 oz*) cuttlefish, diced
4 shrimp, U10 size
sea salt, to taste
14g (*0.5 oz*) parsley, minced
red vein sorrel to garnish, optional
4 lemon wedges

4 slices ciabatta bread
170g (*6 oz*) saffron aioli
For the Saffron Aioli
88ml (*3 fl oz*) white wine
4 threads saffron
1 clove of garlic
170g (*6 oz*) mayonnaise

To prepare the dish, start by making the saffron aioli. Soak the saffron for 5 minutes in the white wine. Bring to boil and reduce by 50% and reverse bain marie. Process the saffron liquid with garlic clove, add the mayonnaise and mix.

To make the classic seafood stew, take a medium size shallow pot and heat the olive oil. Add the onion, garlic and fennel. Cook until onion is translucent for 10 minutes. Add tomato and cook for another 5 minutes. Deglaze with white wine and evaporate alcohol. Add shrimp stock with the saffron threads and bay leaf. Bring to simmer and slow cook to reduce the stock by 30%. Season with salt and white pepper. Add the fish into the sauce, sepia and cover. After minutes add clams, mussels and shrimp. Cover. Simmer for 5 minutes. Discard clams and mussels that did not open. Tune it with salt if needed.

To plate and serve, ladle the stew into individual plates, portioning the seafood equally for all the guests. Finish with minced parsley and red vein sorrel. Served with saffron aioli on the side and toasted pieces of ciabatta.

	Bruce Moffett	*Barrington's Restaurant*	Lamb with bread pudding
	Daniel Mondok	*Raven & Rose*	West Cork rabbit
	Bobby Moore	*Barking Frog*	Seared ahi & braised short rib with soy miso emulsion
	Aldo Mora	*Cafe Central*	Chorizo halibut
	Alejandro Morgan	*Lolinda*	Ceviche de pescado
	Masaharu Morimoto	*Morimoto*	Tuna pizza
	Nick Morse	*Rye Restaurant*	Root beer short rib
	Brian Murphy	*Nostrana*	Vongole bianco pizza
	Gordon Naccarato	*Pacific Grill*	Scallops and fried green tomatoes with coconut-creamed corn and avocado lime crema
	Brian Nasajon	*Beaker & Gray Restaurant*	Yellow curry with rice noodles, coconut milk, chinese sausage, crab, and chimichurri

Laurent Manrique - *Cafe de la Presse*
Parnsip and pear soup with bay scallops
Unlock these 250 recipes on the free CHARITABLE BOOKINGS lifestyle app.

CHARLIE PALMER
Aureole

WHOLE ROASTED TRUFFLE CHICKEN

SERVES 2 | PREPARATION TIME 1 HOUR 45 MINUTES + 24 HOURS TO AIR DRY | COOKING TIME 45 MINUTES

Equipment
butchers wire

For the Truffle Butter
450g (*1 lb*) butter, soft
30ml (*1 oz*) truffle oil
salt and pepper, to taste

For the Chicken
1 whole 1.3kg (*3 lbs*) chicken

For the Chicken Brine
2 cups Kosher salt
180ml(*¾ cup*) honey
2.3l (*5 pints*) water
2.4l (*5¼* pints) ice
½ bunch of thyme
½ bunch of rosemary
½ head garlic
½ tbsp coriander seed
½ tbsp fennel seed
¼ tbsp black peppercorns

Make the truffle butter by mixing the butter and truffle oil and season to taste.

To prepare the chicken brine, combine the water, honey and salt. Bring to boil, skim off residue, add aromatics, and steep. Strain over ice.

Next prepare the chicken. Cut off bottom 2 joints of wings and cut out the wishbone. Brine the whole chicken for 1 hour. Pipe the butter under the skin of the breasts and legs, about 113g (*4 ounces*) per bird. Place fingers under the skin and run butter around the entire bird. Truss properly and allow bird to air dry for 24 hours. When ready to cook, bake in oven for 45 minutes at 205°C (*400°F*).

To finish, serve with the herb bouquet and place ½ lemon and four thyme sprigs in the clove of garlic in the cavity.

WALTER PISANO
Tulio

SWEET POTATO GNOCCHI
SERVES 2 | PREPARATION TIME 4 HOURS | COOKING TIME 10 MINUTES

Equipment
food ricer
For the Dish
1.1kg (*2½ lbs*) sweet potatoes
58g (*2 oz*) parmesan, freshly
grated
1 pinch of nutmeg
1 egg, beaten
240g (*2 cups*) all purpose flour

To prepare the dish, boil the sweet potatoes with their skin on for approximately 1 hour or until soft. Drain the potatoes well and push through a food ricer. Add beaten egg, parmesan, nutmeg and seasoning. Incorporate those ingredients until just mixed. Slowly fold sifted flour into mixture; this is imperative in preventing clumps and keeping gnocchi light. After about ½ of the flour is added start to feel the mixture for wetness and resistance when pushing in. Keep adding flour until dough is slightly wet but is still coming away from the bowl. Allow to rest for 10 minutes. Now lightly dust the table then cut about ⅛ of the dough away and roll into a cylinder shape, about ½ inch wide, and cut into 1 inch pieces. Refrigerate dough for two hours.

To cook, drop the gnocchi into boiling water for approximately 2 minutes or until they rise to the top. Cook for an additional 30 seconds. Drain well. Heat butter in the pan until it foams, place the gnocchi in the pan; brown them on each side. To finish, season with cracked black pepper and salt. Place on a tray and finish with mascarpone.

	Benjamin Navarro	*Parc Bistro Brasserie*	Roasted half duck with a l'orange sauce
	Fernando Navas	*Kingside at The Viceroy Hotel*	Cioppino
	Martial Noguier	*Bistronomic*	Nicoise salad
	Giovanni Novella	*Fresco*	Mussels 'in guazzetto'
	Patrick O'Connell	*The Inn at Little Washington*	Carpaccio of herb crusted baby lamb
	Jeff O'Neill	*Barton G.*	Charcoal roasted foie gras with cold smoked thomcord grapes, scorched honey gelato and cardamom charcoal bread
	Jesus Olivares	*Via Real*	Red oak smoked tenderloin
	Alex Olivier	*Area 31*	Seafood coconut chowder
	Galip Ozbek	*Savann Restaurant*	Seafood purse
	Charlie Palmer	*Aureole*	Whole roasted truffle chicken

Foodie fact #16
There are approximately 350 different pasta shapes around the world.

Christophe Mihy - *El Chorro Lodge*
Signature beef strogonoff
Unlock these 250 recipes on the free CHARITABLE **BOOKINGS** lifestyle app.

JENNIFER PUCCIO
Marlowe

LEO'S LOUIE SALAD

SERVES 2 | PREPARATION TIME 30 MINUTES | COOKING TIME 15 MINUTES

For the Salad
120g (½ cup) shredded romaine
42g (¼ cup) fennel, shaved
42g (¼ cup) mache
42g (¼ cup) radishes
2 tbsp tobiko
1 hard boiled egg, sieved
½ a lemon, juice of
salt to taste
140g -280g (½ to 1 cup) of the
Louie Dressing
240g (1 cup) seafood of choice,
such as rock shrimp, crab and
bay shrimp

For the Louie Dressing
840g (3.5 cups) mayonnaise
240g (1 cup) ketchup
42g (¼ cup) grainy mustard
42g (¼ cup) sriracha
140g (½ cup) chives
140g (½ cup) parsley
42g (¼ cup) capers
42g (¼ cup) gherkins
140g (½ cup) sauerkraut
42g (¼ cup) pickled jalapeño
4 hard boiled eggs

To prepare the dish, start by making the salad. Combine the fennel and romaine. Dress with half the lemon juice and salt and arrange on the plate. Dress the mache and radishes with the remaining lemon juice and salt and arrange over the top of the lettuce. Sprinkle with tobiko and the sieved egg. Plate each salad with half of your chosen seafood. Serve with a side of Louie dressing.

To prepare Louie's dressing, combine the first 5 ingredients in a bowl. Put the remainder of the ingredients except for the hard boiled eggs into the food processor and pulse frequently scraping the sides of the bowl until finely diced not pureed. Add the eggs to the food processor and pulse until a small dice is achieved. Add the blended mixture from the food processor to the contents of the bowl and adjust for salt and black pepper.

Plate each salad with half of your chosen seafood. Serve with a side of Louie dressing.

BENJAMIN RIGGS

Salish Lodge & Spa

SKILLET CHICKEN POT PIE

SERVES 4 | PREPARATION TIME 20 MINUTES | COOKING TIME 1 HOUR

For the Dish

226g (½ lb) chicken breast, diced
226g (½ lb) chicken thigh, diced
2 tbsp canola oil
113g (¼ lb) carrots, diced
113g (¼ lb) onion diced
113g (¼ lb) parsnip, diced
113g (¼ lb) celery, diced
75g (2 oz) wild or cremini
mushrooms, diced

1 tbsp garlic, minced
1 tsp rosemary, minced
1 tbsp thyme, picked leaves
½ tbsp sage leaves, chopped
½ tsp black pepper, fresh
ground
60ml (¼ cup) white wine
480ml (2 cup) chicken stock
120ml (½ cup) heavy cream
1 tbsp Dijon mustard

75g (½ cup) frozen peas
57g (¼ cup) butter
30g (¼ cup) flour
1 sheet puff pastry
1 egg yolk

To prepare the dish, preheat an oven to 205°C (400°F) and heat a skillet over a high heat. Add the oil and the chopped chicken, reduce heat to medium. Sear chicken on all sides and add the carrots, onions, parsnip, celery, and mushrooms. Sear vegetables on all sides but keep al dente. Add herbs and garlic, sauté for 10 to 20 seconds until aromatic, then deglaze with wine, using a wooden spoon to scrape up all the bits from the bottom of the pan. Add the stock and bring to a simmer, reduce heat and cover; let simmer for 20 minutes. Add mustard and cream and bring back to a simmer. Dice butter into small cubes and mash into the flour to form a paste. Add the paste to the chicken mixture and simmer until thick. Add peas. Remove from heat and season to taste with Kosher salt.

Paint puff pastry with egg yolk and lay over the top of the pot pie, then bake for 10 to 14 minutes until pastry is golden and puffed.

Serve directly out of the skillet with fresh chopped parsley.

	Deb Paquette	*Etch restaurant*	Tuna ceviche
	Roland Passot	*La Folie*	Wagyu beef with potato and beef tongue pave with nettle purée and pickled pearl onions
	Michael Patria	*Bar Margot at Four Seasons Atlanta*	Grilled Spanish octopus
	Harley Peet	*Bas Rouge*	Roasted rack of lamb
	Guillermo Pernot	*Cuba Libre*	Papas rellenas
	Stefan Peroutka	*1500 OCEAN at the Hotel Del Coronado*	Pan roasted venison
	Walter Pisano	*Tulio*	Sweet potato gnocchi
	Naomi Pomeroy	*Beast*	Laquered duck confit
	Jennifer Puccio	*Marlowe*	Leo's Louie salad
	Yono Purnomo	*Yono's Restaurant*	Bakmi goreng

Foodie fact #17
You burn more calories eating celery than it contains!

Jeff O'Neill - *Barton G.*
Charcoal roasted foie gras with cold smoked Thomcord grapes, scorched honey gelato and cardamom charcoal bread

Unlock these 250 recipes on the free CHARITABLE BOOKINGS lifestyle app.

EDUARDO RODRIGUEZ
Coyote

PAN SEARED DIVER SCALLOPS
SERVES 4 | PREPARATION TIME 30 MINUTES | COOKING TIME 35 MINUTES

For the Orange Butter
360ml (*1½ cup*) fresh orange juice
2 tsp heavy whipping cream
5 tbsp unsalted butter, sliced
salt and freshly ground pepper
For the Scallops and Vegetables
12 jumbo sea scallops
salt and freshly ground pepper
1 Carnival/Graffiti cauliflower
4 heads baby bok choy
6 pieces baby corn

olive oil, for searing
For the Red Jalapeño Chutney
128g (*1 cup*) dried or fresh mango
512g (*4 cups*) red fresno jalapeños
142ml (*½ cup*) rice vinegar
128g (*1 cup*) sugar
1 inch piece ginger, peeled and finely sliced
64g (*½ cup*) lemongrass, chopped

1 tsp olive oil
142ml (*½ cup*) water
2 shallots, sliced
For the Vanilla Crepes
10 eggs
340g (*2½ cups*) all purpose flour
850ml (*3 cups*) whole milk
57g (*¼ cup*) butter, melted
2 tsp vanilla extract

Start by making the orange butter. Simmer the juice in a heavy small saucepan over moderate heat for 25 minutes or until reduced to ⅓ cup. Add the heavy cream and return to a gentle simmer for 5 minutes, then remove from heat. Add the butter a few slices at a time, whisking constantly. Season and set aside in a warm spot, but not on the stove.

To prepare the scallops, place a heavy bottomed large sauté pan over a high heat. Season the scallops with salt and pepper. Drizzle with olive oil. Add 1 tbsp olive oil to heated pan. Add scallops and sear scallops for 2 minutes on each side until golden brown and opaque in the center.

Now prepare the vegetables by blanching the bok choy, cauliflower and baby corn in boiling water for partial cooking, until tender but not soft. Drain and put in cold water if not using immediately.

To make the jalapeño chutney, mix all of the ingredients together in a large sauté pan. Sauté over a medium heat and cook for 25 minutes until reduced.

To make the crepes, mix all ingredients in a blender. Make 2 ounce ladle size crepe in non-stick sauté pan. Serve as photographed.

FRANCO SAMPOGNA
Jema

GRILLED OCTOPUS with smoked potato and chorizo
SERVES 5 | PREPARATION TIME 1 HOUR | COOKING TIME 3 HOURS

Equipment
blowtorch

For the Octopus
1whole octopus of 2kg (*4.4lbs*)
5g (*0.18oz*) of cilantro seeds
285ml (*1 cup*) of white vinegar
black pepper
1 head of parsley
salt

For the Smoked Potato
1kg (*2.2lbs*) Yukon Gold potato
butter
milk
salt
hay for smoking

For the Sauce and Powder
450g (*1lb*) dry chorizo
1 white onion
1.1l (*1 quart*) cream
olive oil
salt

To prepare the dish, start with the octopus by combining all of the ingredients into a big pot of simmering water. Whenever the water is boiling, lower the heat. Cook the octopus for 2 to 3 hours until very tender. Remove the octopus from the water and let it cool inside the fridge. In a pot of water add the peeled Yukon potatoes and cook them until tender. Remove them and drain all of the water. Smoke the potatoes for 5-10 minutes. Pass the potatoes through the food mill. In a pot add the smoked potatoes and season them with butter, milk and salt to make into a purée. Add the purée inside a siphon and let set aside.

To prepare the sauce and powder heat up a pan and add two spoons of olive oil. Add the dry chorizo sliced into small cubes. Two minutes later add the white onions and let it cook for about five minutes. When the onions are caramelized you can add the cream and let it cook until a smooth consistency. Strain the sauce and save the chorizo, through the strainer. With the remaining chorizo, make a powder. Separate the chorizo from the onions and dry it with a paper towel. Set a fryer at 160 °C (*320°F*) and fry until golden brown. Let it dry on a paper towel and mix the chorizo into a powder.

To finish the dish, heat a grill or barbecue and grill your octopus. On a plate, add some potatoes from your siphon, add the octopus to the side and add some sauce around. To serve you can sprinkle some chorizo powder and micro cilantro.

	Jacques Qualin	*J&G Steakhouse*	Caramelized beef tenderloin with glazed carrots and miso-mustard sauce
	Justin Rambo-Garwood	*39 Rue de Jean*	Mussels marinière
	Ashley Rath	*THE GRILL*	Filet peconic
	Guy Reuge	*Mirabelle Restaurant &Tavern*	Spring Colorado lamb chops
	Lulzim Rexhepi	*SeaSalt*	Soy-braised short ribs with carrot-ginger risotto and crispy horseradish
	Tim Richardson	*Hank's Seafood Restaurant*	Seared rare tuna
	Benjamin Riggs	*Salish Lodge & Spa*	Skillet chicken pot pie
	Eric Ripert	*Le Bernardin*	Dungeness 'Crab Cake' with old bay crisp and shellfish cardamom emulsion
	Waylon Rivers	*Black Sheep 5 Points*	Foie gras torchon with hoshigaki, persimmon purée, rye toast and candied peanuts
	Joe Rodger	*Shift Kitchen & Bar*	Kalimotxo braised short rib with celery, soubise and smoked blue cheese

Foodie fact #18
Mickey Mouse was the first ever
cartoon character to talk when
he said "Hot Dog" in 1929.

Alex Olivier - *Area 31*
Seafood coconut chowder
Unlock these 250 recipes on the free CHARITABLE **BOOKINGS** lifestyle app.

SIR BRUNO SERATO
Anaheim White House

POACHED SALMON AU CHOCOLAT
SERVES 2 | PREPARATION TIME 30 MINUTES | COOKING TIME 15 MINUTES

For the Salmon
450g (16oz) fresh salmon
1 small carrot, chopped
½ onion, chopped
28ml (1oz) lemon juice
2.2l (½ gallon) water
salt

For the White Chocolate Mashed Potato
450g (1lb) Russet potatoes, cleaned and peeled
113g (4oz) white chocolate
57g (2oz) unsalted butter
pinch of salt

For the Citrus Sauce
113g (4oz) unsalted butter
1 whole shallot, diced
140ml (½ cup) orange liqueur
113g (4oz) heavy whipping cream
360ml (1½ cups) of orange juice

To prepare the dish, combine the water, carrot, onion, lemon juice and salt in a large pan and bring to a simmer. Add the salmon and simmer for 12 minutes. Boil the potatoes until soft, then drain. Using a double-boiler, melt the white chocolate. Add the melted chocolate to the potatoes and mash. Add butter and salt and continue to mash until the texture is consistent.

For the sauce, melt 28g (1oz) of butter in a sauté pan and cook the shallots for 2 minutes. Add the orange liqueur and reduce by half. Add the orange juice and reduce by half again. Add the remaining butter and cream and cook until the butter is melted.

To finish, remove the salmon from the pan, place it on top of the mashed potatoes and then top with the citrus sauce.

CAMERON SHAW
Giardina's

CAMERON'S SHRIMP AND GRIT CAKES
SERVES 2 | PREPARATION TIME 1 HOUR 30 MINUTES | COOKING TIME 10 MINUTES

For the Dish
8 jumbo shrimp; peeled and deveined
32g (¼ cup) red, yellow and green bell peppers, finely chopped
1 tbsp green onions
285ml (1 cup) heavy cream

113g (⅓ cup) Louisiana hot sauce
600g (3½ cups) grits
285ml (1 cup) chicken stock
285ml (1 cup) whole milk
272g (2 cups) flour
Old Bay seasoning, to taste
salt and pepper, to taste
oil, for frying

To prepare the dish, bring the chicken stock, whole milk and water to a boil in a heavy saucepan. Add the grits and continue to simmer, stirring occasionally, over a medium heat until the grits are cooked and thick (*approximately 15 to 20 minutes*). Pour into a 9 x 13 pan. Cover and freeze for 1 hour.

Cut the grit cakes to the desired shape. In a bowl, toss the grit cakes in flour, salt and pepper. In a sauté pan or skillet, heat oil to 175°C (*350°F*). Fry until golden brown on both sides, about 5-6 minutes total. In a large skillet, sauté the shrimp over a medium heat, approximately 3 to 4 minutes. Add tri-peppers, green onions, heavy cream, Old Bay seasoning, salt and pepper. Reduce heat to medium-low until thickened.

To finish, pour the shrimp sauce over the fried grit cakes, then garnish with parsley.

	Bill Rodgers	*Keens Steakhouse*	Mutton chop
	Eduardo Rodriguez	*Coyote*	Pan seared diver scallops
	Melissa Rodriguez	*Del Posto*	Girella Genovese with heritage pork and pecorino Toscano
	Kerri Rogers	*Bellwether*	Crispy skin steelhead trout
	Laetitia Rouabah	*Benoit New York*	Delicate corn velouté with crispy lump crab
	Michael Rozzi	*1770 House*	Hand-cut fettuccine with heirloom cherry tomato sauce
	Rob Rubba	*Hazel*	Gnocchi bokki
	Ryan Rupp	*Siena*	Bigeye tuna with burrata, charred avocado and toybox tomato
	Morris Salerno	*Bistecca*	Bacon wrapped scallop
	Jimmy Salomone	*Parsnip Restaurant*	Kombu-cured hamachi with coconut jasmine rice, nori jam, mushroom conserva, ginger and cilantro

Foodie fact #19
An egg contains every vitamin except for vitamin C.

Michael Patria - *Bar Margot at Four Seasons Atlanta*
Grilled Spanish octopus
Unlock these 250 recipes on the free CHARITABLE **BOOKINGS** lifestyle app.

MICHAEL SICHEL
Galatoire's Restaurant

TROUT MEUNIÈRE AMANDINE
SERVES 6 | PREPARATION TIME 25 MINUTES | COOKING TIME 45 MINUTES

For the Dish
420g (*3 cups*) almonds, sliced
2 large eggs
1 pint whole milk
salt and freshly ground black
pepper, to taste

6 x 200g (*8 oz*) speckled trout
filets, cleaned and boned
272 (*2 cups*) all-purpose flour
4.5l (*1 gallon*) vegetable oil
1 meunière butter
3 medium lemons, wedges

To make the dish, preheat the oven to 150°C (*300°F*).

Place the almonds in a pan and toast them in the oven for 15 to 20 minutes, opening the oven to check them every 5 minutes while they cook. When they become golden brown, remove from the oven and set aside.

Make a wash by whisking the eggs and the milk. Season with salt and pepper. Season the trout fillets with salt and pepper and dust with flour. Submerge the floured trout in the egg wash. Gently remove the filets from the egg wash and allow the excess to drip off. Put the filets back into the flour, then gently shake off the excess flour.

Cook the fish in a large, heavy-bottomed pot after heating the oil to 175°C (*350°F*). Test the readiness of the oil by sprinkling a pinch of flour over it. The flour will brown instantly when the oil has reached the correct temperature. Add the trout and fry for 4 to 5 minutes. Remove the fish when the crust is golden brown.

To serve, top each fried trout fillet with almonds and warmed meunière butter. Garnish with lemon wedges and serve at once.

YOSHIHARU SOGI
Zina Lounge

SEARED TUNA
SERVES 4 | PREPARATION TIME 20 MINUTES | COOKING TIME 15 MINUTES

For the Dish
680g (*24oz*) tuna, sushi grade
For the Ume Strawberry Salsa
113g (*4oz*) strawberry
2 tsp ume paste
½ tsp green onion, chopped
1 tsp parsley, chopped
½ tsp black olive, chopped
½ tsp extra virgin olive oil

For the Soy Cranberry Sauce
57g (*2oz*) fresh cranberry
57g (*2oz*) sugar
2 tbsp cranberry juice, 100%
1 tbsp soy sauce
57g (*2oz*) broccoli (*Romanesco*)
57g (*2oz*) sugar snap peas
1 tbsp butter
1 tbsp cooking oil
salt and pepper
micro greens and edible flowers

To prepare the dish, cut the tuna into a 170g (*6oz*) log. Season with salt and pepper. Trim the broccoli and snap peas. Chop the strawberry to small dice and place into a mixing bowl. Add the ume paste, olive, green onion and parsley and stir lightly. Place the cranberry and sugar in a small sauce pot then boil. Turn down to low heat to reduce to approximately 1/3 and lightly thicken. Remove from heat and cool down a little. Transfer into a blender, add the cranberry juice and soy sauce and blend together. Strain with a fine mesh strainer then save by the range to keep warm.

Preheat a frying pan or skillet on high heat until smoking. Add the cooking oil to the seared tuna for a few seconds on all sides then remove from heat and rest a little. Boil the water in a medium size sauce pan. Add salt in the water to cook the broccoli and snap peas so that they are still a little crunchy, then remove from the water. Toss with the butter and season with salt and butter as needed.

Slice the tuna and dish up on plate with the sauce, salsa and vegetables. Garnish and serve.

	Franco Sampogna	*Jema*	Grilled octopus with smoked potato and chorizo
	Noah Sandoval	*Oriole*	Rye capellini with yeast butter and truffles
	Efren Sandoval	*Scoma Restaurant*	Scoma's lazy man's cioppino
	Zach Sato	*Hotel Wailea Relais and Chateax*	Kanpachi lau lau
	Alvin Savella	*The Banyan Tree*	Huli huli chicken
	Gavin Schmidt	*The Morris*	Charred broccolis with grilled squid and chili lime
	Luke Senderling	*Whiskey Kitchen*	Chicken & dumplings
	Sir Bruno Serato	*Anaheim White House*	Poached salmon au chocolat
	Jeremy Sewall	*Row 34*	Fall vegetable hash with baked salmon
	Cameron Shaw	*Giardina's*	Cameron's shrimp and grit cakes

Foodie fact #20
The world's most expensive spice is saffron.

Lulzim Rexhepi - *SeaSalt*
Soy-braised short ribs with carrot-ginger risotto and crispy horseradish
Unlock these 250 recipes on the free CHARITABLE BOOKINGS lifestyle app.

ETHAN STOWELL
Staple & Fancy Mercantile

GNOCCHETTI with pancetta and chanterelles
SERVES 4 | PREPARATION TIME 30 MINUTES | COOKING TIME 20 MINUTES

For the Dish

26g (*0.9 oz*) dried gnocchetti sardi
340g (*12 oz*) fresh chanterelle mushrooms
30ml (*1 fl oz*) extra virgin olive oil, plus more for drizzling
226g (*8 oz*) pancetta, small dice
3 medium cloves of garlic, thinly sliced
pinch of chili flakes
2g (*0.08 oz*) fresh mint, chopped
2g (*0.08 oz*) fresh parsley, chopped
Parmiagiano Reggiano, for serving
Kosher salt
freshly ground pepper

To cook the pasta, bring a large pot of salted water to a rolling boil. Add the pasta and cook for about 12 minutes, or 1 minute less than the package directs. While the pasta is cooking, clean the mushrooms and slice off the rough end of each stem. Quarter the large mushrooms and halve the others. Any tiny chanterelles may be left whole. Set aside.

Heat the olive oil in a sauté pan over a medium heat. Add the pancetta and sauté until some of the fat renders and the pancetta is golden, which should take about 5 minutes. Avoid it becoming too crisp. Add the mushrooms and sauté for around 5 minutes, stirring occasionally to prevent sticking. When the mushrooms are golden, add the garlic and cook for a minute longer. Add the chili flakes.

When the pasta is ready, drain and add to the mushroom-pancetta mixture, adding a couple of tablespoons of cooking water if the mixture seems dry. Season to taste with salt and pepper. Add the mint and parsley and toss.

To serve, tip the pasta into a serving bowl and drizzle with olive oil. Using a vegetable peeler, shave a few large curls of Parmiagiano Reggiano on top.

JOHN STROPKI
Cru Uncorked

ROASTED HALIBUT with sauce verjus
SERVES 4 | PREPARATION TIME 30 MINUTES | COOKING TIME 1 HOUR

For the Fish
4 centre cut skinless halibut portions, 225g (*4 oz*) each
60ml (*2 fl oz*) grapeseed oil
57g (*2 oz*) sweet butter
25g (*0.9 oz*) Marcona almonds, coarsely chopped
salt, to taste

For the Sauce
235ml (*8 fl oz*) chicken stock, reduced by half
60ml (*2 fl oz*) verjus blanc
15ml (*0.5 oz*) heavy cream
80g (*2.8 oz*) sweet butter
25g (*0.9 oz*) golden raisins, soaked in chia tea to rehydrate

15g (*0.5 oz*) capers
salt and white pepper
For the Brown butter glace
236ml (*8 fl*) oz veal stock
50g (*1.75 oz*) reserved brown butter
a few drops of verjus blanc
salt, to taste

As you season the fish, place a sauté pan over a medium high heat and add oil. Wait until it shimmers then add the fish on what would have been skin-side-up. Cook undisturbed until you can see a golden crust developing around the bottom edges. Without turning the fish, place into an oven pre-heated to 180°C (*356°F*) until a knife can easily pierce it. It should take about 5-8 minutes, depending on thickness. When done, flip the fish over and add butter to the pan. Baste, then place onto a resting rack.

Prepare the sauce verjus in a small pan, by heating 50g (*1.75 oz*) of butter until it is light amber and smells nutty. Strain. Reserve 50g (*1.75 oz*) for the veal glace. Combine 28g (*1 oz*) of brown butter along with the remaining butter, chicken stock, cream and verjus. Reduce the sauce to nappe consistency. Optionally, you may add a pinch of xanthan gum to further emulsify. Add the raisins and capers and adjust the seasoning.

To prepare the brown butter glace, combine all in a small sauce pot and reduce to nappe.

To serve, place the fish on a plate and top with some verjus sauce. Drizzle over the fish some brown butter glace and top with almonds.

	Ryan Shearer	*The Hotel Donaldson (HoDo Resturant)*	Braised pork cheeks with caramelized white chocolate sauce
	Chris Shepherd	*Underbelly*	Cha ca style snapper
	Michael Sichel	*Galatoire's Restaurant*	Trout meunière amandine
	Dushyant Singh	*Artizen*	Sea bass with heirloom cannellini beans ragout, pancetta and chermoula
	Dayn Smith	*Houndstooth*	Pan roasted Chesapeake rockfish with lobster beurre blanc, black truffle risotto, julienne fennel, carrot and leek, and braised romaine
	Stephen Smith	*Albion River Restaurant*	Grilled rack of lamb
	Greggory Smith	*Surfing Deer*	Scallops with grilled squash, sweet onion quinoa and pistachio harissa
	Chris Smith	*Callaway Garden*	Spinach stuffed pork chops
	Yoshiharu Sogi	*Zina Lounge*	Seared tuna
	Gerald Sombright	*Ario*	Seared octopus with fried green tomato

Eric Ripert - *Le Bernardin*
Dungeness "Crab Cake" with old bay crisp and shellfish cardamom emulsion
Unlock these 250 recipes on the free CHARITABLE **BOOKINGS** lifestyle app.

BILL TELEPAN
Oceana

LOBSTER BOLOGNESE

SERVES 4 | PREPARATION TIME 45 MINUTES | COOKING TIME 35 MINUTES

For the Dish
2.5kg (5½-6 lb) lobster
250ml (8.5 fl oz) chicken stock
or water
1 shallot, minced
2 cloves of garlic, minced
60ml (2 fl oz) extra virgin olive oil
1.4kg (3 lb) canned tomatoes,
squeezed dry and chopped

very finely
125ml (4.25 fl oz) white wine
30ml (1 fl oz) white wine vinegar
185ml (6.25 fl oz) white lobster
or chicken stock
2 tbsp butter
500g (1.1 lb) spaghetti
2 tbsp minced herbs, preferably
tarragon, chervil, parsley, dill

and/or chives

To prepare the dish, ask your butcher to break apart the lobster into head, claws and tail. Separate the tail and claws from the head and set aside. Open up the head by pulling down the bottom leg-half away from the top. Scrape away and discard the feathery lungs and insides from the head, using a chef's knife. Chop the head into small pieces. Place the heads in a pot with the stock and bring to a simmer, cooking for 15 minutes. Set aside for 15 minutes, then strain and serve.

To cook the dish, bring a pot of water to a rolling boil. Add enough vinegar to flavour the water and add salt to taste, so that it tastes of the sea. Let the water return to a rolling boil and add the lobster, tail and claws. Reduce the heat so that it is medium and cook uncovered. Watch carefully and do not let the water come to a boil again. The pot should bubble occasionally but not simmer. Cook the lobster tail for 5 minutes and the claws for 7 minutes. Remove from the liquid and cool. Shell the tail, knuckles and claws.

Sweat the shallots and garlic in extra virgin olive oil until soft, which will take 7-8 minutes. Add the tomatoes and cook for about 5 minutes. Add the wine and vinegar and reduce until almost dry, which should take 3-5 minutes. Add the stock and bring to a simmer, cooking for 5 minutes. Bring lightly salted water to a boil and add spaghetti. Cook for 7-8 minutes. Drain the spaghetti and add it to the sauce with butter. Cook until the butter is incorporated. Add the warm lobster meat and sprinkle with herbs.

ADAM TIMNEY
Starbelly

STARBELLY'S BACON-JALAPEÑO SPAGHETTI
SERVES 4 | PREPARATION TIME 30 MINUTES | COOKING TIME 30 MINUTES

For the Sauce
1.2kg (*6 cups*) canned whole peeled tomatoes in sauce
60ml (*¼ cup*) olive oil
120g (*½ cup*) onion, minced fine
1 clove of garlic, minced
1 tbsp tomato paste
1 tsp dried thyme
1 tsp dried oregano

For the Spaghetti
500g (*1 lb*) dry or fresh spaghetti
280g (*10 oz*) slab bacon, small cubes
2 jalapeños, sliced, you can remove the seeds to make it less spicy
70ml (*2-3 oz*) white wine
1 tbsp garlic, coarsely chopped

12 basil leaves
parmesan, to garnish

To make the dish, start by using a heavy bottom pot and heating the olive oil over a low heat for a minute, then add and sauté the onions, garlic, thyme, and oregano. Cook until onions are soft, translucent, and fragrant. Add tomato paste and stir to combine. Set aside. Meanwhile, remove whole tomatoes from sauce. Reserve sauce. Add onion mixture to tomatoes and purée in blender, or use an immersion blender, for a mixture that is as coarse or fine as desired. Add puréed tomato mixture back to sauce.

To make the spaghetti, boil the pasta as per manufacturers' instruction then set aside. In a large sauté pan, render bacon until brown and a little crispy over medium heat. Add the jalapeños and garlic and sauté briefly. Remove extra fat from the pan. Add the white wine and reduce by half, then add the prepared tomato sauce and cooked spaghetti. Wilt in fresh basil, mix all together, and season with salt.

Divide into 4 bowls and garnish with shaved parmesan.

	Cara Stadler	*Tao Yuan Restaurant*	Grilled double soy marinated hanger steak with potato parsnip cake, fried pickled mustard greens, yuzu sour cream and umeboshi mustard
	Steve Stone	*82 Queen*	She crab soup
	Ethan Stowell	*Staple & Fancy Mercantile*	Gnocchetti with pancetta and chanterelles
	John Stropki	*Cru Uncorked*	Roasted halibut with sauce verjus
	John Sundstrom	*Lark*	Farro with mascarpone with red wine braised salsify and black trumpet mushrooms
	Nicholas Tarnate	*Aix en Provence*	Fish fillets with potato scales with melted leeks and beurre rouge
	Nathan Tate	*Boulevardier*	Bacon wrapped country pork pâté
	Bill Telepan	*Oceana*	Lobster bolognese
	Adam Timney	*Starbelly*	Starbelly's bacon-jalapeño spaghetti
	Isaac Toups	*Toups South*	Crab salad

Foodie fact #22
Alliumphobia is the fear of garlic.

Laetitia Rouabah - *Benoit New York*
Delicate corn veloute with crispy lump crab
Unlock these 250 recipes on the free CHARITABLE BOOKINGS lifestyle app.

ISAAC TOUPS
Toups South

CRAB SALAD
SERVES 4 | PREPARATION TIME 20 MINUTES

For the Coconut Lime Dressing
1 can of coconut milk
2 limes, juice and zest
5 tsp white sugar
2 Thai chilis
1 tsp salt
6 tbsp basil
28g (*1 oz*) ginger, minced

For the Crab Salad
450g (*1 lb*) jumbo lump crab, picked through for small shells
85ml (*3 oz*) coconut lime dressing
12 green seedless grapes, sliced thin
1 tsp Aleppo pepper
1 head of butter lettuce, or similar
Kosher salt, to taste

extra virgin olive oil

Start the dish by preparing the coconut lime dressing. Combine all of the ingredients in a blender and process for 30 seconds. Set aside.

To prepare the crab salad and serve, take a mixing bowl and combine the crab and dressing carefully, so as not to break up the crab. In a separate bowl, toss the lettuce with a small amount of olive oil and Kosher salt.

Plate the greens and crab salad. Sprinkle evenly with Aleppo pepper.

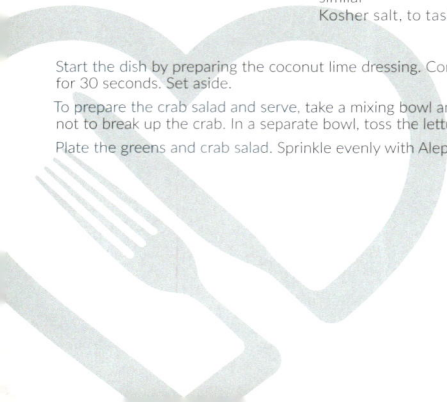

FABIO VIVIANI
Siena Tavern

PROSECCO BRAISED CHICKEN with sun-dried tomatoes and leeks
SERVES 4 | PREPARATION TIME 15 MINUTES | COOKING TIME 20 MINUTES

For the Dish
900g (*2 lbs*) boneless chicken thighs
280g (*1 cup*) flour
1 leek, white and light green parts only, halved and sliced thin
4 garlic cloves, minced
43g (*⅓ cup*) sliced sun-dried tomatoes
1 lemon, sliced
140ml (*½ cup*) prosecco
280ml (*1 cup*) chicken broth
5 tbsp butter
2 tbsp fresh tarragon, minced
2 tbsp Italian parsley, chopped
olive oil
salt and pepper

To prepare the dish, season the chicken with salt and pepper. Drizzle olive oil into a large Dutch oven on a medium heat, enough to barely cover the bottom. Dredge the chicken in flour on the skin side, then place into oil skin side down. Cook the chicken on the skin side for 1 to 2 minutes, then add the leeks. Cook for 3 minutes more, then flip the chicken. Add the garlic and sun-dried tomatoes and season with salt and pepper. Cook for another 2 minutes and add lemon deglazed with prosecco, then add the chicken broth. Bring to a boil and reduce to a simmer. Simmer until liquid has almost reduced, about 5 minutes. Once reduced, turn heat to low and swirl in the butter to complete the sauce. Add tarragon and parsley and adjust seasoning with salt and pepper.

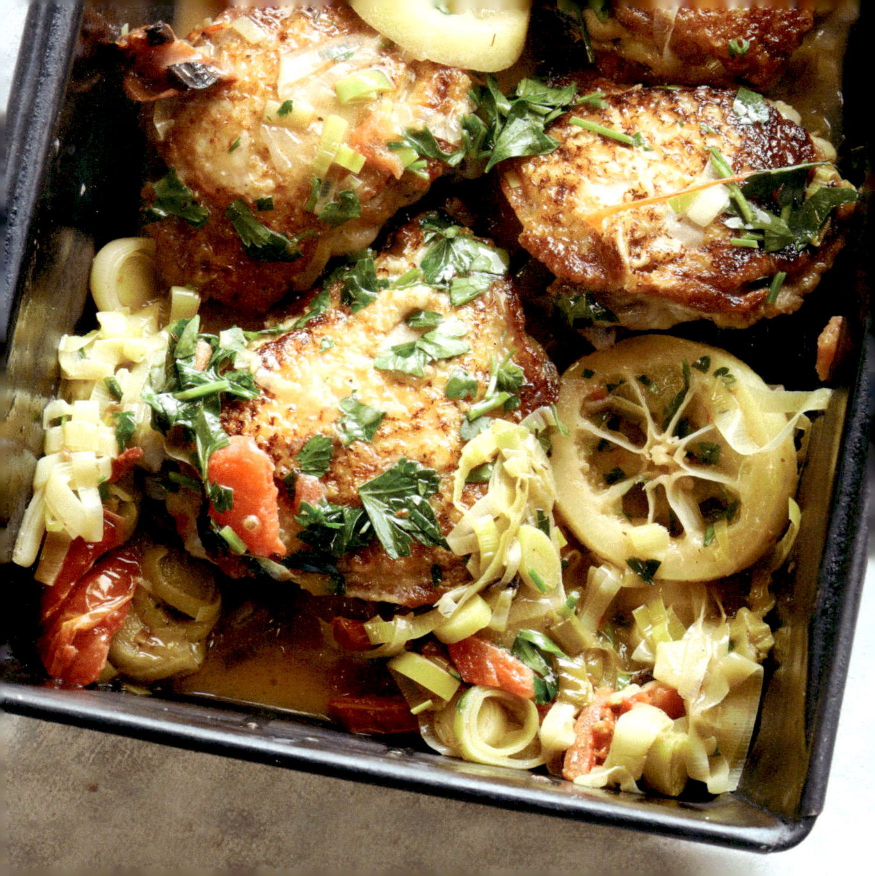

Laurent Tourondel	*LT Steak & Seafood at The Betsy South Beach*	Press tuna
Daniel Traimas	*Cobalt*	Sunchoke leek soup
Andy Trousdale	*Le Bistro*	Bee pollen crusted goat cheese
Peter Ungar	*Tasting Counter*	Gremolata dumplings
Marcellino Verzino	*Marcellino Ristorante*	Lamb chop
David Viana	*Heirloom Kitchen*	Duck breast
Fabio Viviani	*Siena Tavern*	Prosecco braised chicken with sun-dried tomatoes and leeks
James Waller	*Cote D'Azur*	Wild fresh day boat scallops
Ross Warhol	*Oliver's Restaurant*	Scallop tartare
Soichiro Watanabe	*Zenkichi*	Buta no kakuni

Foodie fact #23
The process of carbonating water (infusing water with carbon dioxide) was invented by Englishman Joseph Priestley in 1767.

Rob Rubba – *Hazel*
Gnocchi bokki
Unlock these 250 recipes on the free CHARITABLE **BOOKINGS** lifestyle app

SOICHIRO WATANABE
Zenkichi

BUTA NO KAKUNI
SERVES 4 | PREPARATION TIME 3 HOURS 30 MINUTES | COOKING TIME 2 HOURS

For the Dish
800g (*28 oz*) pork belly
1.3l (*4½ cups*) water
140ml (*½ cup*) mirin
2.2l (*8 cups*) sake
67g (*⅓ cup*) sugar
75ml (*¼ cup*) light soy sauce
1 piece ginger, sliced into long,
flat cuts
1 bunch of scallions, cut into
2inch lengths

To prepare the dish, butcher the pork belly into 200g (*4 oz*) pieces, square, approximately 2 inches thick. Heat the oil in a heavy skillet to a medium-high heat. Brown the pork belly on all sides. Put the pork belly into a bath of water, mirin, sake, ginger and scallions and bring to a simmer for approximately 1.5 hours.

Simmer and frequently skim the surface for excess oil and fat. Add the soy sauce and sugar and bring to boil for 2 minutes. Remove the entire pot from the heat and let it cool down; store for 3 hours.

Reheat and serve over rice with boiled egg, assorted vegetables and arashi (*Japanese mustard*).

MICHELLE WEAVER
Charleston grill

CHARLESTONE GRILL CRABCAKE
SERVES 4 | PREPARATION TIME 5 MINUTES | COOKING TIME 10 MINUTES

For the Dish
450g (*1 lb*) crab meat
1 egg white
½ a lemon, juiced
1 tbsp chives
1 tbsp fresh thyme
115 g (*½ cup*) mayonnaise
2 tbsp bread crumbs made from
fresh, crust-less white bread in
a food processor
salt and freshly ground white
pepper

For the Sauce
6 shrimp, peeled, deveined and
cut into julienne strips
10 red pear tomatoes
10 yellow pear tomatoes
2 limes, juiced
2 shallots, chopped fine
2 tbsp fresh dill
120ml (*½ cup*) extra virgin
olive oil

To prepare the dish, start with the crab. Mix together the mayonnaise, salt, pepper, egg white, zest, juice, chives and thyme. Fold in the crab meat. Make a patty, dust with bread crumbs and sear in butter or oil.

Now make the sauce by heating the shallots in oil, then adding the shrimp and cooking. Add the remaining ingredients and heat through.

Serve warm over crab cakes. Garnish with lemon or lime.

	Derik Watson	*Bistro 82*	Grilled calamari
	Michelle Weaver	*Charleston grill*	Charlestone grill crabcake
	Jim Weaver	*Tre Piani*	Garden state panzanella salad
	Danny Wells	*Republic Restaurant*	Ancient grains salad
	Michael White	*Vaucluse*	Tuna niçoise tartine
	Andrew Whitney	*Virago*	Wagyu tataki
	Andrew Wicklander	*D'Amico's The Continental*	Yellow tail carpaccio
	Martin Woesle	*Mille Fleurs*	Soup of butternut squash with cinnamon croutons
	Lee Wolen	*Boka*	Heirloom carrots with sesame, buttermilk and dates.
	Dennis Wong	*Le Soleil*	Shaken Beef (*Bo Luc Lac*) with onion ring tower and Chinese chives

Foodie fact #24
Most Wasabi eaten is in fact just dyed horseradish.

Zach Sato - *Hotel Wailea Relais and Chateax*
Kanpachi lau lau
Unlock these 250 recipes on the free CHARITABLE **BOOKINGS** lifestyle app.

MICHAEL WHITE
Vaucluse

TUNA NICOISE TARTINE
SERVES 4 | PREPARATION TIME 1 HOUR | COOKING TIME 45 MINUTES

Equipment
microplane grater

For the Tuna
450g (*1 lb*) Bigeye tuna, in a 1 inch piece.

For the Potato Salad
150g (*⅓ lb*) Yukon Gold potatoes, peeled and small dice
285ml (*10 fl oz*) white vinegar
285ml (*10 fl oz*) water
salt, to taste
100g (*3½ oz*) mayonnaise
extra virgin olive oil
lemon juice

For the Olive Tapenade
70g (*2½ oz*) Castelvetrano olives
70g (*2½ oz*) Nicoise olives
1 shallot, medium minced
1 clove of garlic, microplaned
2 lemons, zested
130g (*4½ oz*) canned, peeled tomatoes
1 pinch black pepper, ground

Start the dish by making the potato salad. Peel the potatoes and cut them into marble-sized pieces. Place in a pot, cover with the vinegar and water and add a pinch of salt. Simmer until tender and cool in the liquid. Drain the cooled potatoes and mix with just enough mayonnaise to coat them and bind them together. Mash the potatoes slightly, mix well, finish with a splash of olive oil and taste for seasoning. Add salt and lemon as needed.

For the olive tapenade, place both types of olives in a sauce pan and cover with plenty of cold water. Bring to a boil, drain, rinse well, and drain again. Add the olives to the bowl of a food processor and pulse until they are small-dice size. Add the rest of the ingredients and pulse to combine.

To prepare the tuna, pre-heat a grill or grill pan. Lightly coat the outside of the tuna with olive oil sprinkle with salt. Grill the fish on all sides, about 2 minutes per side, until it is nicely marked and the fish has turned opaque on the outside. Allow the fish to cool fully, and slice into ⅓inch slices. The fish should be rare. Reserve in the refrigerator.

To assemble and serve the dish, slice a loaf of country bread into 1 inch thick slices, drizzle with olive oil and toast in until lightly golden brown. Spread the potato salad over the toasted bread, top with a smear of the olive tapenade, and arrange a quarter of the tuna slices on top. Finish with a drizzle of extra virgin olive oil, a sprinkle of Maldon salt, and Arugula or fresee leaves.

ANDREW WHITNEY
Virago

WAGYU TATAKI
SERVES 04-JUN | PREPARATION TIME 10 MINUTES + 2 HOURS TO REST | COOKING TIME 30 MINUTES

For the Dish
225g (*8 oz*) center cut striploin, preferably highly marbled. Use waguy if available, or prime if not
1 tsp Kosher salt
1 tsp coarse black pepper
14g (*0.5 oz*) butter

14g (*0.5 oz*) beech mushrooms, or any other mushroom
several small radishes, thinly sliced, or micro radish if available
14ml (*0.5 oz*) soy sauce
pickled grape tomatoes, sliced in half length wise

For the Pickled Tomatoes
500g (*1 pint*) grape tomatoes
85ml (*3 oz*) soy sauce
28ml (*1 oz*) water
40g(*1.5 oz*) rice wine vinegar
7g (*0.25 oz*) sugar
salt
clove of of garlic, thinly sliced

To prepare the dish, start with the pickled tomatoes. Combine all of the ingredients, with the exception of the tomatoes, then set aside, slice the tomatoes lengthwise and mix in. Let sit for two hours.

To prepare the beef, liberally season the meat with salt and pepper. Heat a pan and add a small amount of cooking oil. Sear the beef hard on all sides and allow to rest. While the beef is resting, turn the pan to a low medium heat and add the mushrooms and butter. Cook until slightly browned. Drain the mushrooms and season with a pinch of salt.

To finish and plate, slice the rested beef against the grain as thinly as possible and lay flat on the plate. Garnish with radish, mushroom and tomatoes, then drizzle with pickling liquid.

	Mathew Woolf	*Rainbow Room*	Clam "shell" chowder
	Smail Yaakoubi	*Prado*	Paella a la Valenciana
	Roy Yamaguchi	*Roy's Waikiki*	Roy's misoyaki butterfish
	Takashi Yamamoto	*Suzuki*	Miso marinated grilled cod fish
	Basil Yiu	*The Saloon at Dunton Hot Springs*	Smoked char siu pork coppa with spiced cauliflower and black sesame purée
	Alexander Yoon	*Little Fish Byob*	Pan roasted Red Snapper with rosemary cream, fennel and lacinato kale
	Jon Young	*Fresh*	Blue corn chile rellenos with roasted garlic pinon cream sauce and red chile cream
	Hilda Ysusi	*Broken Barrel*	Fish and shrimp ceviche
	Michael Zachman	*Powder at Waldorf Astoria Park City*	Guajillo rubbed buffalo tenderloin
	Andrew Zimmerman	*Sepia*	Coal roasted oysters with ssamjang butter

Foodie fact #25
The tall chef's hat is called a torque.

Dayn Smith - *Houndstooth*
Pan roasted chesapeake rockfish with lobster beurre blanc, black truffle risotto, julienne fennel, carrot and leek, and braised romaine

Unlock these 250 recipes on the free CHARITABLE **BOOKINGS** lifestyle app.

ANDREW WICKLANDER

D'Amico's The Continental

YELLOW TAIL CARPACCIO

SERVES 4 | PREPARATION TIME 45-60 MINUTES

For the Dish
280g (*10 oz*) yellow tail snapper
85ml (*3 oz*) meyer lemon
vinaigrette
65g (*½ cup*) of the pickled
shallot, ginger and scallion
57ml (*2 oz*) extra virgin olive oil
65g (*½ cup*) heirloom tomato,
sliced
57g (*¼ cup*) jalapeño, sliced

very thin
petite cilantro, to taste
sea salt and black pepper
For the Pickled Shallots
2 shallots, sliced
28g (*1 oz*) ginger, julienne
28g (*1 oz*) scallion, thinly sliced
230ml (*8 oz*) Champagne
vinegar
115ml (*4 oz*) water

113g (*4 oz*) granulated sugar
1 tsp salt
**For the meyer lemon
vinaigrette**
2 tbsp meyer lemon juice
½ tbsp granulated sugar
½ tbsp fresh thyme leaves
2 tbsp grapeseed oil
½ tbsp extra virgin olive oil
½ tbsp blood orange-infused
avocado oil, optional

To prepare the dish, make the vinaigrette by mixing the lemon juice, sugar and thyme and slowly whisk in the oil. Season with salt and pepper to taste.

Now make the pickled shallots. In a small pot add the Champagne vinegar, water, sugar and salt. Whisk together until the sugar has dissolved. Bring the liquid to a boil, take off from the heat and add the shallots, ginger and scallion. Let the mixture cool down to room temperature.

To serve, slice the snapper into bite size pieces. Lightly pound out slices and arrange on plates. Sprinkle fish slices with some sea salt and fresh cracked black pepper. Top each plate of fish with 1½ tbsp of meyer lemon vinaigrette and 1 tbsp extra virgin olive oil. Spread the pickled shallot mixture evenly onto the snapper. Arrange the heirloom tomato slices and jalapeño slices on top. Finish with petite cilantro.

SMAIL YAAKOUBI
Prado

PAELLA A LA VALENCIANA
SERVES 4 | PREPARATION TIME 10 MINUTES | COOKING TIME 20 MINUTES

Equipment
paella pan
For the Dish
70ml (*¼ cup*) olive oil
225g (*½ lb*) chorizo
500g (*1lb*) chicken, cut into pieces
500g (*1lb*) large shrimp, peeled
1 whole lobster

250g (*½lb*) mussels
1 small yellow onion, chopped
2 garlic cloves, minced
½ tsp saffron threads, dried and crushed
1 tsp dried oregano
1 tsp smoked paprika
4 tomatoes, peeled, seeded and chopped

65g (*½ cup*) sweet peas
65g (*½ cup*) red bell pepper
1.1kg (*4 cups*) chicken stock
250g (*2 cups*) Bomba rice or any risotto rice
chopped fresh parsley
lemon
salt and pepper to taste

To prepare the dish, take a paella pan and place it over a medium high heat. Warm the olive oil. Season the chicken and chorizo with salt and pepper and add to the hot oil. Brown well then remove the meat from the pan and set aside.

Add the onion, garlic and tomatoes to the hot pan and cook, stirring occasionally until softened, 2 to 3 minutes. Return the chicken and chorizo to the pan, add the stock and simmer for 10 minutes.

Add oregano, paprika, saffron and rice and stir to the mix. Reduce the heat to medium and cook, uncovered, without stirring, until the rice is nearly tender, about 20 minutes. Tuck the shrimp, mussels and lobster into the rice during the last 5 minutes of cooking. Let the paella stand, covered, for 5 to 10 minutes so the rice absorbs all the liquid.

Garnish with parsley lemon wedges and serve immediately.

Recipe Index

MEAT

GAME

POULTRY

CHICKEN

Coq au vin	36
Sunchoke soup	48
Whole roasted truffle chicken	108
Skillet chicken pot pie	116
Prosecco braised chicken with sun-dried tomatoes and leeks	152
Paella a la Valenciana	170
Tortellini di vitello con prosciutto e piselli	32

DUCK

Peanut butter and jelly foie gras	66

QUAIL

Quail egg with brown butter hollandaise and fried leek	30

FISH

BASS

Pan seared alamosa striped bass	60
Cioppino	104

BRANZINO

Branzino dish	38

HALIBUT

Cebiche classico	90
Ceviche de pescado	98
Roasted halibut with sauce verjus	140

SALMON

Salmon crudo	84
Poached salmon au chocolat	126

SEABASS

Black sea bass with cobalt and dragon carrots, and grapefruit	24

SOLE

Sole petite grenobloise	72

TROUT

Trout meuniere amandine	132

TUNA

Sushi grade ahi tuna tartar	42
Seared tuna	134
Tuna nicoise tartine	162

YELLOWTAIL SNAPPER

Yellow tail carpaccio	168

SHELLFISH

CALAMARI

Grilled octopus and calamari	74

CLAM

Vongole bianco pizza	102
Cioppino	104

CRAB

Leo's Louie salad	114
Crab salad	150
Charlestone grill crabcake	158

CUTTLEFISH

Cioppino	104

LOBSTER

Lobster bolognese	144
Paella a la valenciana	170

MUSSEL

Cioppino	104
Paella a la valenciana	170

OCTOPUS

Grilled octopus and calamari	74
Grilled octopus with smoked potato and chorizo	122

PRAWN

Citrus marinated prawns	96
Leo's Louie salad	114

SCALLOP

Soft egg	78
Seared sea scallops	92
Pan seared diver scallops	120

SEA URCHIN

Uni ice cream	68

SHRIMP

Cioppino	104
Cameron's shrimp and grit cakes	128
Paella a la valenciana	170

VEGETARIAN

VEGETARIAN

Cauliflower soup	44
Grilled asparagus on fondued leeks with shaved cashew cheese	56
Butternut squash soup	80
Lucy garden crudité	86

NON-VEGETARIAN CHEESE DISH

Sweet potato gnocchi	110

Acknowledgements

I would like to thank the following for their invaluable assistance and encouragement in taking this concept and turning it into this beautiful book collection.

We gratefully acknowledge the chefs, restaurants and their teams, agents and PRs in supplying the recipes and images of the dishes and in helping us to support so many good causes.

Thanks to our many supporters who have embraced CHARITABLE **BOOKINGS** including Free Holdings, Gravity Integrated Solutions, Pearl DME, Palladium PR, Relish Publications, Part & Company, Seasoned by Chefs, Camille Percheron, Alexandra Preda-Ralev, Violeta Martinez, Alon Shulman, Charlotte Tyson, Deborah Mack, Francesca Di Belmonte, Kasia Szelagowska, Laragh Chambers, Lucy Self, Michael Korel, Richa Verma, Sophie Elbrick, Blessing Zidyarukwa, Alina Pacurar, Will Rockall, Alp Ozen, Helen Mason-Belshaw, Veronique Cabrol, Mantus Siurkus, Ken Fung, Sultan Malik, Marzena Drewniak, Lina Benfarhat, Susanna Jennens, Duncan Peters, Valerie McLeod and Andy Richardson.

With thanks to the many photographers who have supported the chefs and restaurants by providing them with images including: Eric Haines, Vicky Wasik, MGM Resorts International, Nader Khouri, John Revisky, Aubrie Pick, David Martinez, Amy Harrity, Matt Armendariz. Every effort has been made to acknowledge all the photographers. If you have provided a photo and not been credited, please let us know so we can add you to the next edition.

CHARITABLE BOOKINGS
SIGNATURE DISH
USA

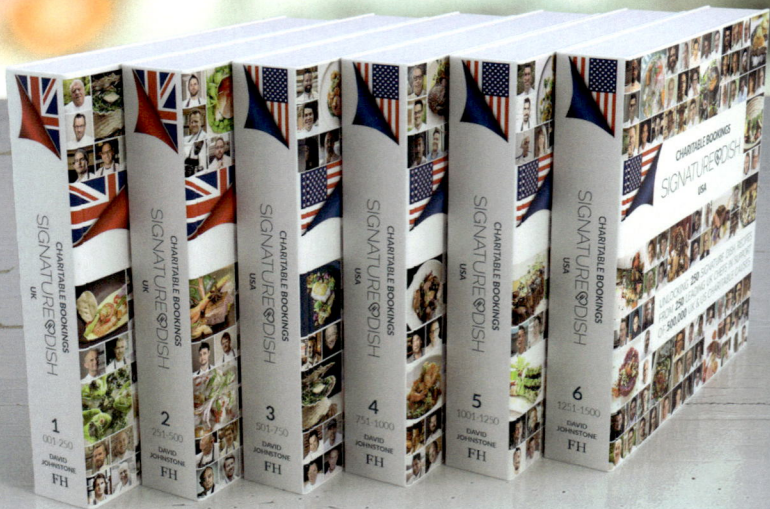

CHARITABLE BOOKINGS SIGNATURE DISH — UK — 1 — 001-250 — DAVID JOHNSTONE — FH

CHARITABLE BOOKINGS SIGNATURE DISH — UK — 2 — 251-500 — DAVID JOHNSTONE — FH

CHARITABLE BOOKINGS SIGNATURE DISH — USA — 3 — 501-750 — DAVID JOHNSTONE — FH

CHARITABLE BOOKINGS SIGNATURE DISH — USA — 4 — 751-1000 — DAVID JOHNSTONE — FH

CHARITABLE BOOKINGS SIGNATURE DISH — USA — 5 — 1001-1250 — DAVID JOHNSTONE — FH

CHARITABLE BOOKINGS SIGNATURE DISH — USA — 6 — 1251-1500 — DAVID JOHNSTONE — FH

MORE BOOKS
IN THE
COLLECTION
AVAILABLE AT

charitable**bookings**.com/**recipe-books**

ISBN: 978-0-9957116-3-1

FH PUBLISHING
Published in London by FH Publishing
fhpublishing.com

9 780995 711631

"The perfect gift for all foodies..."